THE
TOP 100
CHEAP EATS

THE
TOP 100
CHEAP EATS

100 DELICIOUS BUDGET RECIPES FOR THE WHOLE FAMILY

Hilaire Walden

DUNCAN BAIRD PUBLISHERS

LONDON

The Top 100 Cheap Eats
Hilaire Walden

Distributed in the USA and Canada by
Sterling Publishing Co., Inc.
387 Park Avenue South
New York, NY 10016-8810

This edition first published in the UK and USA in 2010 by
Duncan Baird Publishers Ltd
Sixth Floor, Castle House
75–76 Wells Street
London W1T 3QH

Managing Editor: Grace Cheetham
Editor: Alison Bolus
Managing Designer: Suzanne Tuhrim
Commissioned photography: William Lingwood, Simon Smith
 and Toby Scott
Food Stylists: Sunil Vijayakar, Joss Herd and
 Marie-Ange La-Pierre
Prop Stylists: Tessa Evelegh and Helen Trent

Library of Congress Cataloging-in-Publication Data

Walden, Hilaire.
  The top 100 cheap eats : 100 delicious budget recipes for
the whole family / Hilaire Walden.
     p. cm.
  Includes index.
  ISBN 978-1-84483-905-6
  1. Cookery. 2. Low budget cookery. I. Title. II. Title: Top
one hundred cheap eats.
  TX714.W26125 2010
  641.5'52--dc22

                              2009043167

ISBN: 978-1-84483-905-6

10 9 8 7 6 5 4 3 2 1

Typeset in News Gothic
Color reproduction by Colourscan, Singapore
Printed in Malaysia for Imago

For information about custom editions, special sales,
premium and corporate purchases, please contact
Sterling Special Sales Department at 800-805-5489
or specialsales@sterlingpub.com.

Publisher's Note
While every care has been taken in compiling the recipes for
this book, Duncan Baird Publishers, or any other persons
who have been involved in working on this publication,
cannot accept responsibility for any errors or omissions,
inadvertent or not, that may be found in the recipes or text,
nor for any problems that may arise as a result of preparing
one of these recipes. If you are pregnant or breastfeeding or
have any special dietary requirements or medical conditions,
it is advisable to consult a medical professional before
following any of the recipes contained in this book.

Notes on the Recipes
Unless otherwise stated:
Use large eggs, and medium fruit and vegetables
Use fresh ingredients, and fresh herbs
1 tsp. = 5ml 1 tbsp. = 15ml 1 cup = 240ml
• Some of the recipes in this book contain raw or lightly
cooked eggs—these recipes are not recommended for babies
and young children, pregnant women, the elderly, and those
convalescing.

CONTENTS

INTRODUCTION

Eating cheaply doesn't have to mean eating poorly, unimaginatively, and boringly. Cheap food can be just as nutritious, interesting, and delicious as more expensive food, which I hope the recipes in this book prove.

There are many ways you can cut down on food costs. For example, buy basic pantry items, such as pasta, rice, and dried beans, in large packages. Look for special offers, including perishable foods being sold at a reduced price because they are near their "sell by" date. Think before you throw out any food—leftovers from one meal can often be transformed into a second satisfying meal. Look out for reduced items, such as canned tomatoes and beans; any damaged can that is sold is still safe to buy, but it is best to use the contents quickly.

Try to find a market or farm shop and and discover the benefits to buying and eating seasonally. Try your hand at growing your own herbs and some vegetables, too, even if you don't have much of, or any, garden. Pots of herbs can easily be grown on sunny windowsills, and some tomatoes and beans can be grown in grow-bags and even hanging baskets.

The cost of the food is not the only contributing factor in eating cheaply: the costs of preparation and cooking also play their parts. Unless you cook using gas, using pans with dead-flat bottoms that sit snugly on the stovetop are the most economical to use, because they efficiently distribute the heat. Tight-fitting lids also help save money, as does using the most appropriate size of pan for the quantity you are cooking. If you don't have a small enough pan, using a divider lets you cook two vegetables at once. Another way of doubling up is to steam one vegetable in a covered basket over the pan in which you are cooking something else. Instead of boiling vegetables, semi-steam them with just a little water and a pat of butter, in a tightly closed pan. This not only uses less gas or electricity, but also preserves more nutrients.

Above all, buy sensibly, giving some thought to how or when you are going to use the purchase; if you write a menu for the week and just buy what you need, you'll find you save a lot of wastage—and money!

Chapter 1

Appetizers

There are many dishes you can make for a first course without adding much to the overall cost of the meal. Soups are a prime example, such as Chicken & Pearl Barley Soup (see page 10). Soups have the extra plus of filling people up, especially if served with plenty of bread. In fact, serving bread with just about any first course is a useful way to lower people's appetites by a reasonable amount at a modest cost.

It is a good idea to make use of seasonal foods when they are particularly plentiful, such as zucchini, tomatoes, and lettuces in the summer. Another way to save money is to buy pieces of chicken with the bones in and simply remove any bones yourself, if necessary. Or, use chicken wings you have removed from an uncooked whole chicken. With just a few extra ingredients you can make delicious recipes.

Marinated Halloumi Salad (see page 21)

001 Chicken & Pearl Barley Soup

PREPARATION TIME 10 minutes   **COOKING TIME** 50 to 60 minutes   **SERVES** 4

4 to 6 skinless, boneless chicken thighs
1 rosemary sprig
2 bay leaves
5 garlic cloves
scant 1 cup dry white wine
4 cups chicken stock
1 onion, finely chopped

1 carrot, diced
olive oil, for frying
¼ cup pearl barley
½ iceberg lettuce, shredded
2 tbsp. flat-leaf parsley, chopped
salt and freshly ground black pepper
freshly grated Parmesan cheese, to serve

1 Put the chicken, rosemary, bay leaves, 4 of the garlic cloves, wine, and stock into a saucepan. Slowly bring just to a boil, then lower the heat and simmer 10 to 15 minutes, depending on size, until the chicken is just cooked through. Transfer the chicken to a plate using a slotted spoon. Reserve the stock.

2 Chop the reserved garlic clove. Fry the onion, carrot, and garlic in a little oil in a pan over medium heat until soft. Strain in the stock and bring to a boil, then add the pearl barley. Stir and cook 35 to 40 minutes until the barley is tender.

3 Meanwhile, chop the chicken very finely. Add it to the soup with the lettuce and parsley when the barley is cooked. Heat slowly until the lettuce wilts. Season. Serve sprinkled with Parmesan.

002 Chickpea, Pasta & Sage Soup

PREPARATION TIME 10 minutes   COOKING TIME 25 minutes   SERVES 4

1 celery stick, chopped
1 leek, chopped
1 carrot, finely chopped
olive oil, for frying
3 garlic cloves, finely chopped
8 small sage leaves, finely chopped

1 can (15-oz.) chickpeas,
    drained and rinsed
1 can (15-oz.) crushed tomatoes
3½ cups vegetable stock
heaped ½ cup pasta shapes for soup
salt and freshly ground black pepper
freshly grated Parmesan cheese, to serve

1 Fry the celery, leek, and carrot in a little oil in a saucepan over medium heat until light brown.
  Add the garlic and sage and fry 1 minute, then add the chickpeas, tomatoes, and stock.
  Bring to a boil, then lower the heat and simmer 15 to 20 minutes.

2 Meanwhile, cook the pasta in a large pan of boiling salted water following the package
  directions until just cooked, or al dente, and drain well.

3 Pour most of the soup into a blender or food processor and blend to a thick, chunky puree.
  Return to the pan, add the pasta, and heat through, adjusting the thickness, if necessary, by
  boiling so any excess liquid evaporates, or adding more stock if the soup is too thick. Season
  to taste. Serve with the Parmesan.

003 Vegetable & Borlotti Soup

PREPARATION TIME 10 minutes **COOKING TIME** 45 minutes **SERVES** 6

1 onion, chopped
1 small leek, thinly sliced
2 celery sticks, chopped
3 garlic cloves, chopped
3 to 4 thyme sprigs
olive oil, for frying
5 cups vegetable stock
1 can (15-oz.) borlotti beans,
   drained and rinsed

1 zucchini, diced
5 tomatoes, chopped
6 oz. frozen green beans, halved
1 cup frozen fava beans
leaves from a small bunch of flat-leaf
   parsley, chopped
salt and freshly ground black pepper
6 tbsp. homemade or bottled pesto and
   shaved pecorino cheese, to serve

1 Fry the onion, leek, celery, garlic, and thyme in a little olive oil in a large saucepan over medium heat until soft but not colored. Add the stock and bring to a boil, then lower the heat, cover, and simmer 30 minutes.

2 Add the borlotti beans, zucchini, tomatoes, and green and fava beans and return to a boil. Simmer 10 minutes longer, then add the parsley, stir well, and season to taste.

3 Discard the thyme and serve with pesto swirled in and pecorino shavings scattered over.

004 Chicken Satay

PREPARATION TIME 15 minutes, plus 1 to 8 hours marinating   COOKING TIME 20 to 25 minutes   SERVES 4

1½ lb. boneless chicken thighs, cut into
   1-in.-wide strips
squeeze of lemon juice
1 garlic clove, chopped
2 tsp. ground coriander
2 tsp. ground cumin
1 tsp. turmeric
1 tbsp. dark brown sugar
4 tbsp. coconut milk
lemon or lime wedges, to serve

SATAY SAUCE
½ cup unsalted peanuts
1 garlic clove, chopped
2 tbsp. red Thai curry paste
1¾ cups coconut milk
2 tbsp. dark soft brown sugar
squeeze of lemon juice
dash of hot-pepper sauce

1 Put the chicken into a shallow, nonmetallic dish. Sprinkle with the lemon juice.

2 Combine the garlic with the spices, sugar, and coconut milk to make a fairly stiff paste. Rub evenly into the meat. Cover the dish and leave in a cool place at least 1 hour, preferably 8 hours (in which case, put it in the refrigerator, then remove 30 minutes to 1 hour before cooking). Preheat the broiler to high.

3 Meanwhile, make the sauce by toasting the peanuts in a baking pan under the preheated broiler, stirring frequently, so they brown evenly. Transfer to a blender or food processor. Add the garlic, curry paste, and a little of the coconut milk. Mix until smooth, then add the remaining ingredients and mix until evenly blended. Pour into a saucepan. Boil 2 minutes, then lower the heat and simmer 10 minutes, stirring occasionally. If the sauce thickens too much, add water.

4 Thread the chicken onto skewers (soaked if wooden). Cook on a greased broiler rack under the preheated broiler 5 to 10 minutes until the chicken is cooked through.

5 Warm the sauce through, thinning if necessary with a little water, then pour into a warm bowl. Serve the satays with lemon or lime wedges and the sauce.

005 Chicken Yakitori

PREPARATION TIME 10 minutes   COOKING TIME 13 to 15 minutes   SERVES 6

6 boneless chicken thighs, cut into
   1-in. pieces
12 slim leeks, outer leaves removed,
   cut into 1-in. pieces, or 12 fat scallions,
   green parts trimmed and cut into
   1-in. pieces
sunflower oil, for greasing

YAKITORI DIPPING SAUCE
¾ cup dark soy sauce
6 tbsp. saké
6 tbsp. chicken stock
4 tbsp. mirin
1 small garlic clove, finely chopped
4½ tsp. sugar
freshly ground black pepper

1 Preheat the broiler to high. Make the sauce by heating the ingredients in a saucepan over
   medium heat, stirring until the sugar dissolves. Bring to a boil, then lower the heat and simmer
   1 minute. Remove from the heat and leave to cool, then strain.

2 Thread the chicken, skin-side out, and the leeks or scallions alternately onto skewers (soaked
   if wooden).

3 Pour about a quarter of the sauce into a small bowl.

4 Cook the skewers on a greased broiler rack under the preheated broiler 2 minutes, brush with
   the remaining sauce and continue broiling 6 to 8 minutes, basting with the sauce frequently
   and turning once. Serve the skewers with the dipping sauce.

006 Chicken & Rice Noodle Salad

PREPARATION TIME 10 minutes, plus 1 hour marinating   **COOKING TIME** 4 to 5 minutes   **SERVES** 6

8 oz. frozen skinless chicken breast halves,
    thawed and cut into strips
8 oz. rice vermicelli noodles
1 small zucchini, cut into thin strips
3 tbsp. cilantro leaves, coarsely torn
peanut oil, for greasing

MARINADE
1 garlic clove, crushed
1 tbsp. Thai fish sauce
1 tsp. Thai red curry paste
1 tsp. sesame oil
1 tsp. honey

DRESSING
3 tbsp. peanut oil
3 tbsp. lime juice
4½ tsp. Thai fish sauce
few drops of hot-pepper sauce
2 to 3 tsp. sugar

1 Put the chicken strips in a nonmetallic bowl. Make the marinade by combining the
   ingredients. Stir into the chicken, cover, and leave in a cool place 1 hour, stirring occasionally.
2 Meanwhile, pour boiling water over the noodles and leave to soak 4 to 5 minutes, or
   according to the noodle package directions. Drain well and tip into a large bowl. Add the
   zucchini and cilantro.
3 Make the dressing by combining the ingredients. Pour half over the noodles, toss, and then
   leave them to marinate in the refrigerator 1 hour.
4 Preheat the broiler to high. Lift the chicken from the marinade and cook on a greased broiler
   rack under the preheated broiler about 2 minutes on each side.
5 Divide the noodles among four bowls. Pile the chicken on top of the noodles and trickle the
   remaining dressing over.

007 Lime & Honey-Glazed Chicken Wings

PREPARATION TIME 5 minutes, plus 4 to 8 hours marinating   **COOKING TIME** 25 to 30 minutes   **SERVES** 4

12 large chicken wings, tips cut off

lime wedges, to serve

MARINADE

6 tbsp. lime juice

3 tbsp. honey

2 tbsp. olive oil

2 tbsp. dry white wine

2 tsp. marjoram leaves, chopped

1 tsp. thyme leaves

freshly ground black pepper

1 Place the chicken wings in a shallow nonmetallic dish.

2 Make the marinade by mixing all the ingredients together. Pour evenly over the wings, then
   turn them over so they are evenly coated, cover, and leave to marinate in the refrigerator
   4 to 8 hours, turning occasionally. Remove them from the refrigerator 30 minutes to 1 hour
   before cooking.

3 Preheat the oven to 400°F or preheat the broiler. Put the wings on a baking tray and pour any
   remaining marinade over the top.

4 Bake in the preheated oven 25 to 30 minutes or broil for about 10 minutes on each side.
   Remove from the oven or broiler and serve with lime wedges.

008 Herbed Fish Patties

PREPARATION TIME 15 minutes **COOKING TIME** 8 to 10 minutes **SERVES** 6

12 oz. white fish fillets, skinned
1 to 2 tbsp. lemon juice
1 tbsp. Worcestershire sauce
1 tsp. creamed horseradish
½ cup milk
1 tbsp. snipped chives
1 tbsp. chopped parsley

1½ large (12 oz.) cooked potatoes, peeled
  and mashed with a little butter
1 cup fresh bread crumbs
olive oil, for frying
mixed salad leaves, to serve
mayonnaise, to serve

1 Put the fish, lemon juice, Worcestershire sauce, horseradish sauce, and milk in a food processor
  or blender and mix until smooth. Transfer to a bowl and mix in the herbs and mashed potatoes
  until evenly combined.

2 Shape into 6 equal patties. Spread the bread crumbs on a plate and coat the patties evenly in
  the crumbs.

3 Heat a large, nonstick skillet and add the oil. Fry the patties 4 to 5 minutes until golden, then
  turn them over with a pancake turner or metal spatula and fry on the other side 4 to 5 minutes
  longer. Remove from the skillet and drain on paper towels.

4 Serve the fish patties with the salad leaves and some mayonnaise for dipping.

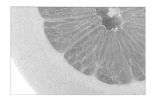  

009 Seared Squid Salad

PREPARATION TIME 10 minutes, plus 2 to 4 hours marinating   COOKING TIME 2 to 3 minutes
SERVES 6

10 oz. frozen prepared small squid, thawed

handful of salad leaves

4 cherry tomatoes, quartered

½ bunch watercress, trimmed

½ cucumber, peeled, halved, seeded,
    and cut into fine strips

2 tbsp. peanut oil

1 tbsp. lime juice

salt and freshly ground black pepper

1 tbsp. cilantro leaves, to sprinkle

MARINADE

1 tbsp. peanut oil

1 tsp. sesame oil

1 tbsp. lemon juice

1 red chili, seeded and finely chopped

1 garlic clove, crushed

sea salt

1 Remove the tentacles from the squid and reserve, then cut the squid bodies lengthwise along
   one side to open them out flat. Using the point of a knife, score diagonal, parallel lines on
   the squid bodies, but do not cut through. Put into a nonmetallic bowl with the tentacles.

2 Combine all the marinade ingredients and pour over the squid. Stir everything together,
   cover, and leave to marinate in the refrigerator 2 to 4 hours.

3 Lift the squid from the marinade and cook in a preheated griddle pan 2 to 3 minutes,
   turning frequently, until chargrilled and cooked, but still tender.

4 Meanwhile, toss the salad leaves, tomatoes, watercress, and cucumber
   together. Trickle the peanut oil and lime juice over to moisten. Season.

5 Slice the squid bodies into rings and pile onto the salad.
   Sprinkle with cilantro, then serve.

010 Bean, Herb & Goat Cheese Frittata

PREPARATION TIME 10 minutes **COOKING TIME** 15 to 20 minutes **SERVES** 3 to 4

¾ cup drained canned cannellini beans, rinsed

4 eggs, lightly beaten

2 garlic cloves, finely chopped

2 tbsp. flat-leaf parsley, chopped

olive oil, for frying

3 oz. goat cheese, finely chopped or crumbled

2 well-flavored tomatoes, chopped

2 tsp. balsamic vinegar

1 tbsp. shredded basil leaves

1½ tbsp. freshly grated Parmesan cheese

salt and freshly ground black pepper

1 Stir the beans into the eggs with the garlic, parsley, and seasoning.

2 Heat a thin film of oil in a 7½- to 8-inch skillet over high heat, pour in the egg mixture, and spread it out evenly. Cook over medium–low heat 10 to 15 minutes until most of the mixture is set but the top is still creamy. Preheat the broiler to high.

3 Scatter the goat cheese over the top and cook under the preheated grill 5 minutes until the cheese is bubbling.

4 Meanwhile, combine the tomatoes with the balsamic vinegar and basil.

5 Sprinkle the Parmesan over the frittata and serve in wedges, accompanied by the tomatoes.

011 **Marinated Halloumi Salad**

PREPARATION TIME 10 minutes, plus 1 to 4 hours marinating   **COOKING TIME** 4 minutes   **SERVES** 6

12 oz. halloumi cheese, cut into
   ½-in.-thick slices
1 tbsp. salted capers, well rinsed and dried
12 mixed black and green olives, pitted
flat-leaf parsley leaves, to scatter
lemon wedges, to serve

MARINADE
½ cup extra-virgin olive oil
1 tsp. Dijon mustard
2 tsp. balsamic vinegar
1 tbsp. thyme leaves
pinch of sugar
1 red chili, seeded and finely chopped

1 Lay the cheese slices in a shallow, nonmetallic dish.
2 Combine the marinade ingredients and pour over the cheese. Turn the slices over, cover the
  dish, and leave in a cool place 1 to 4 hours, turning the slices occasionally.
3 Lift the cheese from the marinade and cook in a dry, nonstick skillet 2 minutes on each side,
  turning carefully with a metal spatula until golden.
4 Transfer to plates, scatter the capers, olives, and parsley over, and serve immediately with
  the lemon wedges.

012 Spaghetti with Sun-Dried Tomatoes, Garlic & Chilli

PREPARATION TIME 5 minutes   **COOKING TIME** 12 minutes   **SERVES** 6

14 oz. spaghetti

12 to 14 sun-dried tomatoes in oil,
   drained and sliced

3 garlic cloves, finely chopped

1 tbsp. flat-leaf parsley, chopped

pinch of dried chili flakes

¼ cup extra-virgin olive oil

1 Cook the spaghetti in a large saucepan of boiling salted water following the package directions until just cooked or, al dente, and drain well

2 Meanwhile, combine the remaining ingredients in a small pan and warm over low heat.

3 Toss the spaghetti with the sauce and serve.

013 Bulgar-Stuffed Peppers

PREPARATION TIME 10 minutes   **COOKING TIME** 25 to 30 minutes   **SERVES** 4

3 tbsp. bulgar wheat

2 large red bell peppers, halved, seeded, and stem ends removed

2 tbsp. milk

2 tbsp. soft cheese with garlic and herbs

2 eggs, beaten

1 well-flavored tomato, peeled, seeded, and chopped

2 tbsp. flat-leaf parsley, chopped

6 tbsp. freshly grated Parmesan cheese

1 Preheat the oven to 350°F.

2 Pour boiling water over the bulgar and leave to soak, but don't let it to become too soft. Drain off the excess water thoroughly, if necessary.

3 Meanwhile, bring a pan of water to a boil. Add the pepper halves and blanch 3 minutes. Leave upside down on a dish towel to drain completely.

4 Stir the milk into the soft cheese until smooth, then mix in the eggs, bulgar, tomato, and parsley.

5 Stand the pepper halves in a shallow baking dish or pan, propping them upright with crumpled foil, if necessary. Spoon in the wheat mixture. Sprinkle the Parmesan over and bake in the preheated oven 20 to 25 minutes until the filling is just set. Do not overcook.

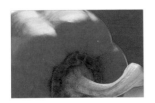

014 Spinach-Filled Tomatoes with Mozzarella

PREPARATION TIME 10 minutes   **COOKING TIME** 15 minutes   **SERVES** 4

4 large plum tomatoes, halved lengthwise
2 tsp. olive oil, plus extra for greasing
1 shallot, finely chopped
1 garlic clove, finely chopped

6 oz. frozen spinach, thawed and
  squeezed dry
2 to 3 oz. mozzarella cheese, sliced
salt and freshly ground black pepper

1 Carefully scoop the pulp from the tomatoes. Turn the shells upside down, and leave to drain. Chop the tomato flesh.
2 Heat the oil in a small nonstick skillet, add the shallot and garlic, and fry over medium heat until soft, stirring occasionally. Add the chopped tomato flesh and heat, stirring, until the moisture evaporates. Stir in the spinach, season, and heat through. Preheat the oven to 350°F.
3 Stand the tomato halves in a greased baking pan, cut-side up. Pack the spinach mixture into the hollows and top with a slice of mozzarella.
4 Cook in the preheated oven 20 to 25 minutes. Do not let the tomatoes become too soft otherwise they will be difficult to transfer to plates.

015 Broiled Tomato Bruschettas

PREPARATION TIME 5 to 10 minutes   **COOKING TIME** 6 minutes   **SERVES** 2 to 4

4 sun-ripened tomatoes, halved
olive oil, for brushing
1 large ciabatta, halved lengthwise
4 tbsp. bottled tapenade
1 tbsp. extra-virgin olive oil

1 Peppadew (bottled mild pepper piquante),
    drained and thinly sliced
small handful (about 10) basil leaves
salt and freshly ground black pepper

1 Preheat the broiler to high. Brush the tomatoes with olive oil, season, and cook on a broiler rack under the preheated broiler 6 minutes, turning once.

2 Meanwhile, cut each length of ciabatta in half widthways and toast under the broiler with the tomatoes. Remove from the broiler rack and spread the cut sides of the toast with the tapenade.

3 Squash the tomatoes onto the ciabatta. Trickle the extra-virgin olive oil over the tops and sprinkle with the Peppadew and basil leaves.

016 Green Caesar Salad

PREPARATION TIME 10 minutes   **COOKING TIME** 5 minutes   **SERVES** 4 to 6

1 large romaine lettuce, torn into pieces

CROUTONS
5 tbsp. olive oil
2 to 3 slices of country bread, crusts
    removed, cut into ½-inch cubes
2 garlic cloves, lightly crushed

DRESSING
1 egg yolk
2 tsp. wholegrain mustard
5 tbsp. olive oil
3 garlic cloves, finely chopped
2 tbsp. red-wine vinegar
4 to 6 tbsp. freshly grated Parmesan cheese
3 anchovy fillets, drained and chopped
freshly ground black pepper

1 To make the croutons, heat the oil in a skillet, add the bread cubes and the garlic, and fry until crisp and light brown. Transfer to paper towels to drain.

2 Make the dressing by mixing the egg yolk with the mustard, then slowly pour in the oil, whisking until it is all incorporated. Add the garlic, vinegar, Parmesan, anchovy fillets, and plenty of black pepper. Whisk until thoroughly mixed.

3 Just before serving, put the lettuce leaves into a bowl. Pour the dressing over and toss to combine, then add the croutons and toss once more.

017 **Marinated Zucchini with Lemon & Mint**

PREPARATION TIME 10 minutes   **COOKING TIME** 3 to 5 minutes   **SERVES** 4 to 6

1 lb. small zucchini, quartered
lengthwise and halved
2 tsp. olive oil
4 scallions, white parts only,
finely chopped
small mint leaves, to scatter

DRESSING
5 tbsp. extra-virgin olive oil
2 tbsp. lemon juice
1 garlic clove, chopped
1 tbsp. mint leaves, chopped
pinch of sugar
salt and freshly ground black pepper

1 Put the zucchini in a bowl and toss with the olive oil.

2 Cook the zucchini in a griddle pan 3 to 5 minutes until lightly charred and soft, turning once.

3 Meanwhile, make the dressing by whisking the ingredients together with seasoning to taste.

4 Transfer the zucchini to a bowl and stir in the dressing, then cover with plastic wrap and leave
20 minutes, until cool.

5 To serve, add the scallions, adjust the seasoning, and scatter with the mint leaves.

Chapter 2

FISH & SEAFOOD

Many varieties of fish have become expensive, but that does not mean you have to eliminate fish from your diet. Instead of going for the most-popular varieties, such as cod and haddock, look for cheaper types, such as pollock and catfish (don't be put off by the slightly grayish color of their flesh, as they become white when cooked). When they are combined with interesting flavorings, such as Thai spices (see page 40), most people will be hard-pressed to guess you had been saving money on the fish.

Make the most of any bargains you come across. If you see a side of salmon at a reduced price, for example, you can cut it into individual portions and freeze. And unless you want perfect slices of smoked salmon for presentation's sake, buy smoked salmon trimmings, which are a fraction of the price and perfect for pasta dishes, such as the one on page 34.

Seafood Linguine Baked in Paper (see page 49)

018 Salmon Shells with Pesto & Tomato Sauce

PREPARATION TIME 5 minutes, plus optional overnight resting and making the sauce
COOKING TIME 20 to 35 minutes   **SERVES** 4

1 can (7-oz.) salmon, drained

scant ½ cup ricotta cheese

2–3 tsp. finely grated lemon zest

16 large pasta shells

2 tbsp. homemade or bottled pesto

2 well-flavored tomatoes,
  seeded and chopped

⅔ recipe quantity Béchamel Sauce,
  (see page 90), kept warm

salt and freshly ground black pepper

1 Combine the salmon with the ricotta, lemon zest, and seasoning. Cover and leave overnight, if time allows, to let the flavors develop.

2 Preheat the oven to 375°F.

3 Cook the pasta in a large saucepan of boiling salted water following the package directions but for one minute less than the suggested time. Drain well, then leave upside down on a clean dish towel to drain completely.

4 Divide the salmon mixture among the shells and place, open side up, in a shallow baking dish. Cover tightly with foil and place in the preheated oven 15 to 20 minutes to warm through.

5 Add the pesto and tomatoes to the béchamel sauce and stir well. Pour the sauce over the shells, and serve.

019 Salmon Fishcakes

PREPARATION TIME 15 minutes, plus 2 to 3 hours cooling and chilling and making the sauce
COOKING TIME 20 to 30 minutes   SERVES 4

1 lb. skinless salmon fillet
1½ large (12 oz.) Idaho potatoes
small pat of unsalted butter
1 to 2 tbsp. chopped dill, to taste
juice and finely grated zest of ½ large lemon
seasoned all-purpose flour, for shaping

2 eggs, beaten
heaped 2 cups fresh bread crumbs
olive oil, for frying
salt and freshly ground black pepper
1 recipe quantity Red Pepper & Tomato
   Sauce (see page 54), hot, to serve

1 Put the salmon in a skillet with barely enough water to cover. Season and bring to a boil.
  Remove the pan from the heat, cover, and leave the salmon to cool in the liquid 1 hour.
  Drain off the liquid. Skin the salmon and flake the flesh into a bowl.

2 Meanwhile, cook the potatoes in a saucepan of boiling salted water 10 to 15 minutes until
  tender. Drain well, then add the butter and mash.

3 Add the salmon, dill, lemon juice and zest, and seasoning to the mashed potatoes and, with
  well-floured hands, form the mixture into 4 patties.

4 Tip the beaten eggs onto one shallow dish and the bread crumbs onto a plate. Coat the patties
  in the egg, allowing the surplus to drain off, then coat in the bread crumbs, patting them firmly
  in place. Cover and chill 1 to 2 hours.

5 Heat a little olive oil in a skillet and fry the fishcakes over medium heat 4 minutes on each
  side until golden, turning them carefully with a pancake turner or metal spatula. Remove and
  drain well on paper towels.

6 Serve the fishcakes with the pepper and tomato sauce on the side.

020 Teriyaki Salmon

PREPARATION TIME 5 minutes, plus 1 to 2 hours marinating   **COOKING TIME** 4 to 5 minutes   **SERVES** 4

4 salmon steaks, about 6 oz. each
vegetable oil, for greasing the broiler rack
lightly toasted sesame seeds, lightly
   crushed, to sprinkle

MARINADE
2 tbsp. mirin
2 tbsp. soy sauce
2 tbsp. saké
2 tsp. grated fresh gingerroot
1 garlic clove, pressed through a garlic press
½ to ¾ tsp. Sichuan peppercorns, ground

1 Place the salmon steaks in a nonmetallic dish.
2 Make the marinade by mixing all the ingredients together. Pour over the salmon and turn the steaks over so they are evenly coated, then cover and leave in a cool place 1 to 2 hours, turning occasionally. (If marinating in the refrigerator, remove the salmon 30 minutes before cooking to allow it to come to room temperature.)
3 Preheat the broiler to high. Lift the steaks from the marinade. Reserve the marinade.
4 Cook the salmon on a greased broiler rack under the preheated broileer about 2 minutes. Brush with the reserved marinade, turn the steaks over, brush again with the marinade, and cook 2 minutes longer, or until the salmon is cooked to your liking. Sprinkle the salmon with the sesame seeds before serving.

021 Couscous with Salmon, Fava Beans & Parsley

PREPARATION TIME 10 to 15 minutes **COOKING TIME** 1 minute **SERVES** 4

2¼ cups couscous
1 cup fresh or frozen fava beans, thawed
olive oil, for frying
2 garlic cloves, finely chopped
15 oz. canned salmon, drained and flaked

4 tbsp. chopped flat-leaf parsley
about 4 tbsp. lemon juice
freshly grated pecorino cheese, to serve
  (optional)

1 Put the couscous in a bowl, cover with water according to the package directions, and leave 5 to 10 minutes, adding the fava beans at the same time.

2 Meanwhile, heat a little olive oil in a small pan and fry the garlic over low heat 1 minute. Add to the couscous and fava beans and stir in the salmon, then toss with the parsley and lemon juice to taste. Serve with pecorino, if desired.

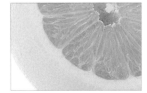

022 Green & White Tagliatelle with Smoked Salmon, Spinach & Lemon

PREPARATION TIME 5 minutes **COOKING TIME** 10 to 12 minutes **SERVES** 4

14 oz. green and white tagliatelle

14 oz. spinach leaves, torn into small pieces

small pat of unsalted butter

juice and finely grated zest of 1 lemon

1 cup crème fraîche

6 oz. smoked salmon trimmings, cut into strips

salt and freshly ground black pepper

snipped chives, to sprinkle

1 Cook the pasta in a large saucepan of boiling salted water following the package directions until just cooked, or al dente, pushing the spinach into the water 30 seconds before the end of the cooking time. Drain well.

2 Meanwhile, melt the butter in a small saucepan. Whisk in the lemon juice and zest, the crème fraîche, and seasoning and warm through. Toss with the pasta, spinach, and smoked salmon. Serve sprinkled with the chives.

023 Tuna & Broccoli Bake

PREPARATION TIME 10 minutes   **COOKING TIME** 35 to 40 minutes   **SERVES** 4

1 lb. 4 oz. potatoes, halved or quartered, depending on size
2 cups small broccoli florets
7 oz. canned tuna, drained and flaked
1 large (or 2 halves) grilled red bell pepper in oil, drained and sliced

1 cup grated Taleggio or Fontina cheese
vegetable oil, for greasing the dish
2½ cups milk
3 eggs, beaten
2 tbsp. fresh bread crumbs
salt and freshly ground black pepper

1 Preheat the oven to 350°F.
2 Cook the potatoes in a saucepan of boiling salted water until tender. Drain well, then, when cool enough to handle, slice thinly. Meanwhile, cook the broccoli in a pan of boiling salted water until just tender, then drain well. Distribute the potatoes, broccoli, tuna, red pepper, and half of the Taleggio in a greased baking dish.
3 Beat the milk with the eggs and seasoning and pour the mixture into the dish. It should flow through the ingredients, but if it does not, ease them apart with a fork. Scatter the remaining taleggio and the bread crumbs over the top, making sure any protruding broccoli is covered.
4 Bake in the preheated oven about 25 minutes until just set and golden.

024 Rosemary-Skewered Pollock

PREPARATION TIME 5 minutes **COOKING TIME** 35 to 40 minutes **SERVES** 6

12 rosemary stems, leaves stripped

1 lb. 7 oz. pollock fillet, skinned and cut
   into chunks

1 tsp. pimentón (smoked paprika)

6 slices firm white bread

sea salt and freshly ground black pepper

lemon wedges, to serve

GARLIC & LEMON BASTE

1 cup olive oil, plus extra for greasing

2 large garlic bulbs, divided into cloves,
   unpeeled

1 lemon, halved and cut into chunks

3 rosemary sprigs

1 To make the baste, put all the ingredients in a saucepan with black pepper and cook over very
   low heat 30 minutes; do not let the oil become too hot or the garlic will fry. Strain off and
   reserve the oil and the garlic.

2 Preheat the broiler to high. Using the rosemary stems as skewers, carefully pierce a hole
   through each chunk of fish. Sprinkle the fish with black pepper and pimentón, then brush with
   the garlic-flavored oil. Thread onto the rosemary "skewers."

3 Cook the fish on a greased broiler rack under the preheated broiler 6 to 8 minutes, turning
   occasionally and brushing with some of the garlic oil, until brown on the edges. Remove the
   skewers from the broiler rack and sprinkle with sea salt.

4 Meanwhile, toast the bread in batches and cut in half diagonally. Using a slotted spoon, lift the
   garlic from the oil and either squash the garlic flesh from the skins on to the toasts, or remove
   the skins and eat the cloves with the fish. Serve the lemon wedges on the side.

025 Haddock with Indian Spices

PREPARATION TIME 10 minutes, plus 1 hour marinating   **COOKING TIME** 6 to 8 minutes   **SERVES** 4

4 haddock fillets, about 7 oz. each

MARINADE
2 tsp. garam masala
1 tsp. ground cumin
½ tsp. cayenne pepper
½ tsp. turmeric
3 tbsp. chopped cilantro
1 to 2 tbsp. peanut oil, plus extra
   for greasing
salt and freshly ground black pepper

RAITA
½ cucumber, seeded
1 small garlic clove, finely chopped
⅔ cup Greek yogurt
2 tbsp. chopped mint
salt and freshly ground black pepper

1 Put the haddock into a nonmetallic dish.

2 Make the marinade by stirring all the ingredients together. Rub into the haddock to coat evenly and thoroughly. Cover the dish and leave in the refrigerator to marinate 1 hour.

3 Preheat the broiler to high. To make the raita, grate the cucumber on the coarse side of a cheese grater. Drain well on paper towels, squeezing out any liquid. Combine the cucumber with the garlic, yogurt, mint, and seasoning. (Cover the dish and chill until required if not serving immediately.)

4 Cook the haddock on a greased broiler rack under the preheated broiler 6 to 8 minutes until cooked through, turning once with a pancake turner or metal spatula. Serve with the Raita.

026 Mexican Whole Fish Burgers

PREPARATION TIME 10 minutes, plus 30 minutes marinating **COOKING TIME** 6 to 8 minutes
SERVES 6

1 lb. 14 oz. thick, firm white fish fillets,
  such as pollock or haddock
1 bunch cilantro, coarsely chopped
1 garlic clove, chopped
1 red chili, seeded and chopped
2 tsp. paprika
1 tsp. ground cumin
finely grated zest of 1 lime
5 tbsp. olive oil

6 hamburger buns or rolls, split
salt and freshly ground black pepper
spinach leaves and red onion slices, to serve

LIME MAYONNAISE
½ cup mayonnaise
2 tbsp. lime juice
dash hot-pepper sauce

1 Cut the fish into 6 pieces that are slightly larger than the buns. Put into a nonmetallic dish.
2 Mix the cilantro, garlic, chili, paprika, cumin, lime zest, and olive oil in a blender. Season
  to taste. Coat the fish evenly with the paste, then cover the dish and leave in a cool place
  30 minutes.
3 Preheat the broiler to high. Meanwhile, mix the lime mayonnaise ingredients together. Adjust
  the seasoning, if necessary.
4 Broil the fish under the broiler on an oiled rack of broil pan 3 to 4 minutes over medium heat
  on each side until cooked through and opaque, turning with a pancake turner or metal spatula.
5 While the fish is cooking, toast the halved buns. Spread some of the mayo on the cut sides
  of the buns, then add some spinach leaves and red onion slices to the bottoms of the buns
  and top with a piece of fish. Cover with the bun tops and serve.

027 Thai Fishcakes

PREPARATION TIME 10 minutes, plus 1 hour chilling   **COOKING TIME** 8 to 10 minutes   **SERVES** 4

1 shallot, coarsely chopped
1 large garlic clove, coarsely chopped
½-in. piece fresh gingerroot, coarsely
  chopped
2 kaffir lime leaves, or 1 tsp. lime zest
1 red chili, seeded and coarsely chopped
2 tbsp. Thai fish sauce
pinch of sugar

1 lb. pollock or catfish fillets, skinned
  and chopped
2 scallions, coarsely chopped
2 tbsp. finely chopped cilantro, plus extra
  to sprinkle
olive oil, for frying
lime wedges, to serve

1 Combine the shallot, garlic, ginger, lime leaves, chili, fish sauce, and sugar in a food processor. Add the fish and process until reduced to a paste.

2 Add the scallions and cilantro. Pulse a few times until combined but not chopped farther.

3 Knead the mixture with your hands until smooth, then form into 1-inch-thick patties. Cover and chill at least 1 hour.

4 Heat a little olive oil in a skillet and fry the fishcakes over medium heat 4 to 5 minutes on each side until golden on the outside but still rare to medium in the middle, turning them carefully with a pancake turner or metal spatula. Remove from the pan and drain well on paper towels. Sprinkle with cilantro and serve with lime wedges.

028 Baked Trout with Fennel & Lemon

PREPARATION TIME 15 minutes   **COOKING TIME** 15 to 20 minutes   **SERVES** 4

1 fennel bulb

2 large trout, about 1 lb. 9 oz. each,
  filleted to give 4 fillets

3 garlic cloves, thinly sliced

2 tbsp. chopped flat-leaf parsley

1 lemon, halved and thinly sliced

1 tsp. fennel seeds

1 tbsp. olive oil

salt and freshly ground black pepper

1 Trim the stems from the fennel bulb, saving the feathery green fronds. Discard the core. Halve
  the fennel bulb and slice thinly. Blanch it in boiling salted water 2 minutes. Drain very well.

2 Preheat the oven to 400ºF.

3 Cut 4 sheets of foil, each large enough to enclose a fillet. Put a quarter of the garlic, sliced
  fennel, and parsley on each sheet of foil, spreading them in an even layer. Lay a fillet on top,
  skin side uppermost. Lay the lemon slices on top. Scatter the fennel seeds and reserved
  feathery fronds over. Season and trickle the oil over the top. Fold the foil loosely over the fish
  and twist the edges together firmly to seal.

4 Place all the packages on a baking sheet and bake in the preheated oven 15 to 20 minutes
  until the flesh flakes easily with a fork.

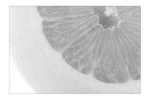

029 Whole Chinese-Style Trout

PREPARATION TIME 10 minutes, plus 2 to 3 hours marinating   **COOKING TIME** 15 to 20 minutes
SERVES 4

4 whole trout, dressed

6 tbsp. grated fresh gingerroot

½ cup rice wine vinegar

6 tbsp. sesame oil

12 scallions, finely chopped

several cilantro sprigs

sea salt and freshly ground black pepper

lime wedges, to serve

1 Cut 2 or 3 slashes in both sides of the fish, cutting right down to the bone. Insert a small amount of the ginger in each slash. Season inside and out and transfer the fish to a large baking dish.

2 Pour the rice wine vinegar and sesame oil over the trout and sprinkle with the scallions. Lay cilantro sprigs on top of and around the fish. Cover with a lid or foil and leave in the refrigerator about 2 hours to marinate, turning the fish over once. Preheat the oven to 350°F. Bring the fish back to room temperature.

3 Cook in the preheated oven 15 to 20 minutes until the flesh in the slashes is opaque. Serve the fish with the cooking juices spooned over and accompanied by lime wedges.

030 Mackerel with Sweet Chili & Mint

PREPARATION TIME 6 minutes   **COOKING TIME** 10 to 15 minutes   **SERVES** 4

4 mackerel fillets, about 7 oz. each,
    dressed
vegetable oil, for greasing

DRESSING
3 tbsp. rice wine vinegar
2 tbsp. sugar
1½ tbsp. chopped mint
1 large red chili, seeded and
    finely chopped
2-in. piece fresh gingerroot,
    finely chopped

1 Preheat the broiler to high.
2 Place the fillets skin-side down and place in a greased, shallow baking dish. Season. Cook
   under the broiler 2 to 3 minutes on each side until the mackerel is cooked through and the
   flesh flakes easily with tested with the tip of a knife.
3 Meanwhile, make the dressing. Whisk the vinegar with the sugar, then stir in the remaining
   ingredients. Serve with the mackerel.

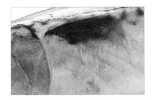

031 **Smoked Fish Pie**

PREPARATION TIME 15 minutes, plus making the sauces   **COOKING TIME** 40 to 45 minutes   **SERVES** 4 to 6

1½ to 2 lb potatoes, halved or quartered, depending on size

5 tbsp. hot milk

4 tbsp. butter, melted

12 oz. frozen spinach, thawed and well drained

small pat of unsalted butter

1 lb. 8 oz. smoked haddock fillet, skinned and cubed

2 tbsp. chopped mixed herbs, such as basil, oregano, thyme, and fennel

1 recipe quantity Béchamel Sauce (see page 90)

1 tbsp. fresh bread crumbs

1 Cook the potatoes in a saucepan of boiling salted water 10 to 15 minutes until tender, then drain thoroughly. Return them to the pan and put low heat a few minutes to dry. Add the milk and butter and mash the potatoes.

2 While the potatoes are cooking, squeeze out the surplus moisture from the spinach. Put in a pan with the unsalted butter and heat through, then spread half over the bottom of a 2½-quart deep baking dish.

3 Preheat the oven to 375°F. Arrange the haddock over the spinach. Stir the herbs into the béchamel sauce and pour over the haddock mixture. Spread the mashed potatoes evenly over the sauce and sprinkle with the bread crumbs. Bake in the preheated oven about 30 minutes until golden and bubbling.

032 Fish Tortillas with Tomato & Cilantro Salsa

PREPARATION TIME 15 minutes   COOKING TIME 6 minutes   SERVES 4

1 garlic clove, crushed to a paste
½ tsp. ground cumin
½ tsp. dried oregano
½ tsp. hot paprika
1 tbsp. lime juice
2 tbsp. olive oil, plus extra for frying
1 lb. 5 oz. pollock fillets
8 soft flour tortillas
½ cup mayonnaise
salt and freshly ground black pepper

SALSA
4 vine-ripened tomatoes, seeded and diced
1 small red onion, finely chopped
2 tbsp. chopped cilantro
1 red chili, seeded and finely chopped
1 tbsp. lemon juice

1 Make the salsa by combing the ingredients in a nonmetallic bowl. Cover and set aside.
2 Mix the garlic with a pinch of salt, some black pepper, the spices, lime juice, and olive oil. Brush the fish with the mixture.
3 Cook the fish in a little oil in a skillet 3 minutes on each side, then transfer to a plate.
4 Meanwhile, warm the tortillas according to the package directions.
5 Flake the fish coarsely with a fork and serve rolled up in the tortillas with the salsa and some mayonnaise.

033 Spiced Sardines with Orange & Olive Salad

PREPARATION TIME 15 minutes, plus 2 to 3 hours marinating   **COOKING TIME** 6 to 8 minutes
SERVES 4

4 garlic cloves, crushed

1 tbsp. olive oil

1 tbsp. lemon juice

1 tsp. ground Sichuan peppercorns

½ tsp. hot paprika

12 to 16 fresh sardines, depending on size,
    dressed

salt and freshly ground black pepper

SALAD

5 oranges

1 small red onion, very thinly sliced

16 large salt-packed black olives, pitted

½ cup flat-leaf parsley leaves,
    coarsely chopped

extra-virgin olive oil, for trickling,
    plus extra for greasing

1 Mix together the garlic, olive oil, lemon juice, peppercorns, paprika, and seasoning.
  Rub thoroughly over the sardines, then cover and leave in a cool place 2 to 3 hours.

2 Preheat the broiler to high. Make the salad by peeling and
  segmenting the oranges, removing all the pith and membranes.
  Put the segments in a bowl with the red onion, olives,
  and parsley. Season and trickle some oil over.

3 Thread the sardines onto pairs of greased parallel skewers,
  alternating the heads and tails, and cook on a greased
  broiler rack under the preheated grill 3 to 4 minutes
  on each side until cooked through and the flesh flakes
  easily. Serve with the orange and olive salad.

034 Spaghetti with Shrimp, Tomatoes & Capers

PREPARATION TIME 10 minutes   **COOKING TIME** 10 to 12 minutes   **SERVES** 4

14 oz. spaghetti

1 onion, chopped

olive oil, for frying

2 garlic cloves, crushed

3½ cups chopped well-flavored plum
   tomatoes

1 tsp. oregano

12 oz. frozen medium raw shelled shrimp,
   thawed

1½ tbsp. salted capers, rinsed, and dried

salt and freshly ground black pepper

1 Cook the spaghetti in a large saucepan of boiling salted water following the package directions
  until just cooked, or al dente.

2 Meanwhile, fry the onion in a little oil in a large skillet over medium heat until soft and
  beginning to color. Add the garlic and fry 1 to 2 minutes. Add the tomatoes and oregano and
  cook over high heat until the juice evaporates, but do not let the tomatoes disintegrate.

3 Add the shrimp to the sauce and cook over low heat about 2 minutes, just until they turn pink.
  Remove the pan from the heat and add the capers and seasoning.

4 Drain the spaghetti, toss with the sauce, and serve.

035 Seafood Linguine Baked in Paper

PREPARATION TIME 5 minutes **COOKING TIME** 30 to 35 minutes **SERVES** 4 to 6

18 oz. linguine

olive oil, for the paper and for frying

2 garlic cloves, crushed

1 can (15-oz.) crushed tomatoes

2 tbsp. sun-dried tomato paste

1 lb. 9 oz. frozen mixed seafood, thawed

1½ to 2 tbsp. capers

leaves from a small bunch of flat-leaf
    parsley, chopped

salt and freshly ground black pepper

1 Preheat the oven to 375°F. Lightly grease 4 or 6 pieces of baking parchment paper, each
    14-inches square.

2 Cook the linguine in a large saucepan of boiling salted water following the package directions,
    but for 1 minute less than the suggested time.

3 Meanwhile, heat a little oil in a saucepan and fry the garlic over low heat 1 minute. Stir in the
    tomatoes, tomato paste, and seasoning, increase the heat, and bring to a boil, then lower
    the heat and simmer, uncovered, 5 minutes.

4 Drain the pasta and toss it and the seafood, capers, and parsley with the tomato sauce.

5 Place one portion in the middle of each piece of parchment paper. Fold the edges loosely
    over the pasta mixture and twist the edges together to seal tightly. Place on a baking sheet
    and cook in the preheated oven 20 to 25 minutes until hot throughout.

036 Fusilli with Mussels, Tomatoes & Chili

PREPARATION TIME 15 minutes   **COOKING TIME** 12 to 15 minutes   **SERVES** 4

14 oz. fusilli

4 tbsp. dry white wine

2 lb. mussels, scrubbed, cleaned,
    and thoroughly rinsed

3 tbsp. olive oil

2 garlic cloves, finely chopped

1 small red chili, seeded and finely chopped

10 oz. cherry tomatoes

leaves from a small bunch of flat-leaf
    parsley, chopped

salt and freshly ground black pepper

1 Cook the pasta in a large saucepan of boiling salted water following the package directions
   until just cooked, or al dente.

2 Meanwhile, put the wine and mussels (discarding any that don't shut when tapped) in a large
   pan, cover, and cook over medium heat 3 to 4 minutes, shaking the pan frequently, until the
   shells open; discard any that remain closed.

3 While the pasta and mussels are cooking, heat the oil in a large skillet and fry the garlic and
   chili over low heat about 2 minutes until soft but not colored. Halve some of the tomatoes,
   then add all the tomatoes to the pan and fry until they just begin to become soft.

4 Remove the shells from half of the mussels, then strain off and reserve the cooking liquid.
   Add the parsley, all the mussels, the reserved cooking liquid, and seasoning to the tomato
   sauce and heat through gently. Drain the pasta, toss with the sauce, and and serve.

037 Spaghetti alla Puttanesca

PREPARATION TIME 5 minutes   **COOKING TIME** 20 minutes   **SERVES** 4

olive oil, for frying
2 garlic cloves, chopped
6 canned anchovy fillets,
   drained and chopped
2 cans (15-oz.) crushed tomatoes

1 lb. spaghetti
1 tbsp. oregano
1 tbsp. capers, rinsed
14 oil-cured pitted black olives, sliced
salt and freshly ground black pepper

1 Heat a little oil in a skillet and fry the garlic over low heat 1 minute, then stir in the anchovy
   fillets until they disintegrate. Add the tomatoes and bring to a boil, then lower the heat and
   simmer about 15 minutes, uncovered, stirring occasionally, until the sauce thickens. Season
   with plenty of black pepper.
2 Meanwhile, cook the spaghetti in a large saucepan of boiling salted water following the
   package directions until just cooked, or al dente, and drain well.
3 Add the oregano, capers, and olives to the sauce, and toss with the pasta.

Chapter 3

POULTRY & MEAT

You'll find frozen meat and poultry is generally much cheaper than the fresh versions, and by using seasonings and flavorings imaginatively, you can make truly delicious dishes. Turkey is a particularly economical buy, and a flavorsome marinade transforms it into a really delicous dish, as shown on page 68, so you can enjoy it at times other than just Thanksgiving.

To make meat and poultry go further, combine them with less-expensive ingredients like legumes. A dish that illustrates how this works is the Sausage & Mushroom Casserole on page 71. Here you can use one can of beans if you are making it for four people but two cans and no extra meat if there are six people to feed. Pasta dishes are also a way of making a little expensive protein go a long way, and they are nearly always popular.

Sausage & Eggplant Lasagne (see page 74)

038 Chicken-Stuffed Pasta Shells

PREPARATION TIME 15 minutes   **COOKING TIME** 45 minutes to 1 hour   **SERVES** 4

3¼ cups sliced button mushrooms
1 onion, finely chopped
1 cup finely chopped zucchini
1 red bell pepper, halved, seeded,
   and finely chopped
olive oil, for frying
4 oz. frozen skinless, boneless chicken
   breast half, thawed and finely chopped
½ cup fresh bread crumbs
2 tbsp. chopped flat-leaf parsley
3 tbsp. chicken stock

16 large pasta shells
salt and freshly ground black pepper

RED PEPPER & TOMATO SAUCE
2 large red bell peppers (about 8 oz. each),
   halved, seeded, and chopped
1 garlic clove, chopped
2 scallions, chopped
2½ cups chopped well-flavored tomatoes
leaves from a small bunch of basil, shredded

1 Fry the mushrooms, onion, zucchini, and pepper in a little oil in a skillet over medium heat, stirring occasionally, until soft. Stir in the chicken and cook 5 minutes longer. Add the bread crumbs, parsley, stock, and seasoning and bring to a boil, then set aside.

2 Cook the pasta shells in a large saucepan of boiling salted water following the package directions, but for 1 minute less than the suggested time.

3 Meanwhile, make the sauce by cooking the peppers, garlic, scallions, and tomatoes in a pan 15 to 20 minutes, uncovered, until thick. Pour into a blender or food processor and blend until almost smooth, or use a stick blender. Add the basil and season.

4 Preheat the oven to 425°F.

5 Drain the pasta shells well. Fill with the chicken mixture and arrange in a single layer in a shallow baking dish. Pour the sauce around. Cover and bake in the preheated oven 15 minutes, or until hot and bubbling

039 Chicken with Lemon & Mustard Sauce

PREPARATION TIME 10 minutes, plus 2 hours marinating **COOKING TIME** 15 to 20 minutes **SERVES** 4

8 chicken thighs

MARINADE
2 large garlic cloves
3 tbsp. Dijon mustard

5 tbsp. olive oil
5 tbsp. lemon juice
½ tsp. dried thyme
salt and freshly ground black pepper

1 Cut slashes in the chicken, then arrange in a single layer in a baking dish.
2 Crush the garlic to a paste with a pinch of salt, using the back of a knife. Mix with the remaining ingredients. Spread evenly over the chicken and turn the pieces over so they are evenly coated, then cover and leave in a cool place for hours, turning occasionally.
3 Preheat the oven to 350°F or the broiler to medium-high. Cook the chicken pieces about 20 minutes, or broil about 15 minutes, turning occasionally, until the skin is golden and the juices run clear when the thickest part is pierced with a skewer.

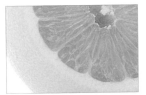

040 Tandoori Chicken Kabobs

PREPARATION TIME 10 minutes, plus 2 hours marinating **COOKING TIME** 10 minutes **SERVES** 4

8 boneless chicken thighs, cut into
approximately 1-in. pieces
vegetable oil, for greasing

MARINADE
scant 1 cup plain yogurt
2 garlic cloves, finely chopped

2 tsp. grated fresh gingerroot
½ red chili, seeded and finely chopped
1 tsp. ground cardamom
1 tsp. ground coriander
1 tsp. garam masala
1 tsp. ground cumin
salt

1 Put the chicken in a shallow, nonmetallic dish.
2 Make the marinade by stirring the ingredients together and season with salt. Pour over the chicken and turn the pieces over so they are coated thoroughly and evenly. Cover the dish and leave to chill 2 hours, turning occasionally.
3 Preheat the broiler to high. Drain the chicken from the marinade and thread onto skewers (presoaked if wooden). Cook the chicken on a greased broiler rack under the preheated broiler about 10 minutes, turning occasionally, until brown and the juices run clear when the thickest part is pierced.

041 Chicken with Ginger, Garam Masala & Coconut

PREPARATION TIME 10 minutes   COOKING TIME 12 to 15 minutes   SERVES 4

olive oil, for frying
1 onion, chopped
4 garlic cloves, crushed
1 tbsp. grated fresh gingerroot
8 boneless chicken thighs or drumsticks,
  cut into bite-size pieces

1 tbsp. garam masala
scant ½ cup coconut milk
1 tbsp. Thai fish sauce
1 small handful cilantro leaves
freshly ground black pepper

1 Heat a little oil in a skillet over low heat and cook the onion and garlic a few minutes until soft. Add the ginger and stir 1 to 2 minutes, then add the chicken. Stir for about 2 minutes, then sprinkle in the garam masala and stir again before mixing in the coconut milk and fish sauce.

2 Season with pepper and bring almost to a boil, then lower the heat and simmer gently, covered, 5 to 7 minutes until the chicken is cooked through. Scatter the cilantro over the dish and serve.

042 Moroccan Chicken with Tabbouleh

PREPARATION TIME 15 minutes, plus 2 to 5 hours marinating   **COOKING TIME** 8 minutes   **SERVES** 4

1 lb. 12 oz. frozen chicken breast halves,
   thawed and cut into 1-in. pieces
2 tbsp. olive oil, plus extra for greasing
5 tbsp. lemon juice
1 large garlic clove, finely chopped
small handful cilantro, finely chopped
small handful flat-leaf parsley, finely chopped
1 tbsp. ground cumin
1 tbsp. cinnamon
1 tbsp. ground coriander
salt and freshly ground black pepper

TABBOULEH
½ cup bulgar
4 oz. Italian mixed peppers in oil,
   drained and chopped
4 tbsp. olive oil
4 tbsp. lemon juice
2 handfuls flat-leaf parsley, finely chopped
8 large sprigs of mint, finely chopped

1 Thread the chicken pieces onto skewers (soaked if wooden) and place in a single layer
in a nonmetallic dish.

2 Combine the olive oil, lemon juice, garlic, herbs, spices, and seasoning. Pour over the chicken
pieces and turn so they are well coated, then cover and leave to marinate in a cool place
2 to 5 hours.

3 Meanwhile, make the tabbouleh by putting the bulgar into a heatproof bowl. Pour scant ½ cup
boiling water over and leave 30 minutes until the water is absorbed, stirring occasionally.

4 Preheat the broiler to high. Fluff up the bulgar wheat with a fork. Stir through the remaining
tabbouleh ingredients and season.

5 Lift the chicken from the dish (reserving the marinade) and cook on a greased broiler rack
under the preheated broiler 4 minutes on each side, brushing with the reserved marinade
occasionally. Using a fork, slip the cooked chicken from the skewers onto the tabbouleh.

043 Turkish Chicken Wraps

PREPARATION TIME 10 minutes, plus 1 to 3 hours marinating   COOKING TIME 14 to 16 minutes
SERVES 4

4 frozen skinless, boneless chicken
  breast halves, thawed
2 garlic cloves
½ tsp. cinnamon
½ tsp. ground allspice
4 tbsp. Greek yogurt
3 tbsp. lemon juice
1 tbsp. olive oil
4 pita breads
salt and freshly ground black pepper

shredded iceberg lettuce and sliced
  tomatoes, to serve

CILANTRO AIOLI
3 garlic cloves, chopped
2 egg yolks
juice of 1 lime, or to taste
1¼ cups peanut oil, plus extra for greasing
small handful cilantro leaves, chopped

1 Put the chicken into a nonmetallic dish. Crush the garlic with a pinch of salt, using the back of
  a knife, then mix with the spices, yogurt, lemon juice, oil, and black pepper. Coat the chicken
  with the mixture. Cover and leave to marinate in a cool place 1 to 3 hours, turning occasionally.
2 To make the aïoli, put the garlic, egg yolks, and lime juice into a blender and mix briefly. With
  the motor running, slowly pour in the oil until the mixture becomes thick and creamy. Season
  and transfer to a bowl. Cover and chill until ready to serve. Stir in the cilantro.
3 Preheat the broiler to medium-high. Lift the chicken from the marinade. Cook on an greased
  broiler rack under the preheated broiler about 7 to 8 minutes on each side. Remove, cover,
  and set aside 5 to 10 minutes before slicing.
4 Meanwhile, warm the pitas under the preheated broiler 30 seconds per side. Split each one
  open and stack the halves on top of each other, cut side uppermost. Divide the lettuce and
  tomatoes over the pita stacks. Lay the chicken on top, add some aïoli, and roll them up.

044 Peking-Style Chicken

PREPARATION TIME 15 minutes, plus 4 to 6 hours marinating   COOKING TIME 45 minutes   SERVES 4

3 lb. 6 oz. frozen chicken breast halves
   on the bone, thawed
1 bunch scallions, sliced
Chinese pancakes, to serve

DIPPING SAUCE
2 tsp. sesame oil
1-tsp. piece fresh gingerroot, grated
½ cup hoisin sauce

GLAZE
2 tbsp. hoisin sauce
2 tbsp. white-wine vinegar
2 tbsp. honey
2 tbsp. mango chutney
1 tbsp. soy sauce
juice of 1 lemon

1 Make the glaze by stirring all the ingredients together in a nonmetallic bowl. Brush evenly and thoroughly over the chicken and place the pieces a single layer in a shallow baking dish. Cover and leave in a cool place 4 to 6 hours, brushing occasionally with any remaining glaze.

2 Preheat the oven to 350°F. Make the dipping sauce by heating the sesame oil in a small saucepan. Add the ginger and cook over low heat 5 minutes. Put the hoisin sauce in a small dish, strain in the oil, and stir to combine.

3 Uncover the baking dish and cook the chicken in the preheated oven about 40 minutes, turning occasionally, until the juices run clear when the thickest part is pierced. Remove from the oven and leave to stand 5 minutes before slicing.

4 Meanwhile, warm the pancakes following the package directions. Serve the sliced chicken, scallions, pancakes, and dipping sauce separately so everyone can assemble their own.

045 Jerk Chicken

PREPARATION TIME 10 minutes, plus 2 hours marinating   **COOKING TIME** 35 minutes   **SERVES** 6

6 whole chicken legs

JERK SAUCE
1 onion, coarsely chopped
½ cup white-wine vinegar
½ cup dark soy sauce

4 tbsp. coarsely chopped fresh gingerroot
leaves from small bunch of thyme
1 to 2 red chilies, seeded and
    finely chopped
½ tsp. ground allspice
freshly ground black pepper

1 Put the chicken in a large, shallow baking dish.
2 Make the jerk sauce by combining the ingredients in a blender until smooth. Pour over the
   chicken and turn the pieces over so they are evenly coated, then cover the dish and leave
   in a cool place 2 hours, turning occasionally.
3 Preheat the oven to 350ºF. Cook the chicken pieces about 35 minutes, turning occasionally,
   until the skin is golden and the juices run clear when the thickest part is pierced with a skewer.

046 Chicken Curry

PREPARATION TIME 10 minutes   COOKING TIME 30 minutes   SERVES 4

olive oil, for frying
1 onion, finely chopped
4 frozen chicken breast halves, thawed

COCONUT SAUCE
2 tsp. cumin seeds
1 red chili, seeded and coarsely chopped
3 garlic cloves, coarsely chopped

½ tsp. salt
1 lemongrass stalk, outer layer removed,
   thinly sliced
1¾ cup coconut milk
2 tbsp. lime juice
3 tbsp. chopped cilantro
3 tbsp. chopped flat-leaf parsley

1 To make the coconut sauce, heat a small dry, heavy-bottom skillet, add the cumin seeds, and heat about 10 seconds until fragrant. Tip into a small blender or food processor, add the chili, garlic, salt, and lemongrass and mix together. Add the coconut milk, lime juice, cilantro, and parsley and process to a smooth sauce.

2 Heat a little oil in the skillet and fry the onion until soft, then add the chicken breasts and seal on both sides. Pour the coconut sauce over the top and bring to a boil, then lower the heat and simmer very slowly, uncovered, 20 to 25 minutes until the sauce is thick and the chicken is cooked through and the juices run clear when the thickest part is pierced.

047 Mushroom-Stuffed Chicken Thighs

PREPARATION TIME 10 minutes, plus 20 minutes soaking the toothpicks **COOKING TIME** 20 minutes
SERVES 4

1 tbsp. unsalted butter

¾ cup finely chopped mushrooms

2 tbsp. cream cheese

1 tbsp. chopped parsley

8 boneless chicken thighs

olive oil, for brushing

salt and freshly ground black pepper

1 Soak 8 to 16 wooden toothpicks in water 20 minutes. Drain and set aside. Melt the butter
  in a skillet and fry the mushrooms over medium heat 5 minutes, or until tender. Using a
  slotted spoon, transfer onto folded paper towels to drain.

2 Preheat the broiler to medium. Mix the mushrooms with the cheese, parsley, and seasoning,
  and use this mixture to stuff the chicken thighs. Secure the thighs closed with toothpicks.
  Brush the thighs with oil and season them.

3 Cook on a greased broiler rack under the preheated broiler 10 to 15 minutes, turning once,
  until brown and cooked through.

048 Fruited Chicken Couscous

PREPARATION TIME 10 minutes **COOKING TIME** 10 to 15 minutes **SERVES** 4

2½ cups vegetable stock, hot

1⅓ cups couscous

8 boneless chicken thighs or drumsticks,
  or a combination of both

3 cups chicken stock

½ cup dried apricots, chopped

⅓ cup raisins

½ cup dried figs, chopped

½ cup toasted slivered almonds

⅓ cup pistachio nuts, lightly toasted

4 tbsp. chopped flat-leaf parsley

2 tbsp. chopped cilantro leaves

1 tbsp. chopped mint leaves

4 tbsp. olive oil

juice and finely grated zest of 1 orange

salt and freshly ground black pepper

Pour the vegetable stock over the couscous in a heatproof bowl, stir with a fork, cover, and leave to cool until the stock is absorbed.

Meanwhile, poach the chicken very gently in the chicken stock in a large saucepan for 10 to 15 minutes until cooked through. Lift the chicken out of the stock, remove the skin, and cut the meat into bite-size pieces.

Fluff up the couscous with a fork, then fork in the fruits, nuts, herbs, and chicken.

Combine the olive oil with the orange juice and zest and salt and black pepper. Whisk until emulsified, then stir into the couscous.

049 Cajun Chicken with Tomato Salsa

PREPARATION TIME 10 minutes, plus 2 to 3 hours marinating   COOKING TIME 15 minutes   SERVES 6

2 tsp. dried thyme
2 tsp. dried oregano
2 tsp. paprika
1 tsp. ground cumin
1 tsp. cayenne pepper
6 frozen boneless chicken breast halves,
   with skin on, thawed
peanut oil, for brushing
salt and freshly ground black pepper
lime quarters, to serve

TOMATO SALSA
4½ cups chopped firm but ripe
   plum tomatoes
1 red onion, finely chopped
1 small red chili, seeded and finely chopped
1½ tbsp. chopped cilantro
1½ tbsp. balsamic vinegar
3 tbsp. olive oil

1 Mix together the herbs, spices, and seasoning. Brush the chicken lightly with oil, then rub the
  spice mixture into the chicken. Cover and leave in a cool place 2 to 3 hours to marinate.

2 Meanwhile, make the salsa by combining the ingredients in a non-metallic bowl. Add salt to
  taste, then cover the bowl and chill until required.

3 Preheat the broiler to medium. Thread the lime quarters onto skewers, if you would like them broile

4 Cook the chicken on a greased broiler rack under the preheated broiler about 15 minutes until
  brown and cooked through, turning once.
  If broiling the limes, cook the skewers
  alongside until caramelized. Serve the
  chicken with the lime quarters, either
  fresh or broiled as above, and
  accompanied by the salsa.

050 Turkey with Garlic, Ginger & Sesame

PREPARATION TIME 10 minutes, plus 4 to 6 hours marinating   **COOKING TIME** 10 to 12 minutes
SERVES 4

4 turkey steaks

MARINADE
3 garlic cloves, finely chopped
2 tbsp. grated fresh gingerroot

½ cup dark soy sauce
1 tbsp. rice wine or medium-dry sherry
1 tbsp. sesame oil
2 tsp. sesame seeds
2 tbsp. dark brown sugar

1 Using the point of a sharp knife, make cuts over the top and bottom of the turkey steaks.
  Lay the steaks in a single layer in a nonmetallic dish.
2 Put the marinade ingredients in a pitcher or bowl and mix to combine, then pour over
  the steaks, turning them over to coat thoroughly. Cover the dish and leave in a cool place
  4 to 6 hours to marinate, turning occasionally.
3 Lift the turkey steaks from the marinade and cook in a preheated griddle pan 5 to 6 minutes
  on each side until the juices run clear when the thickest part is pierced with a skewer.

051 Turkey Tikka Sausages

PREPARATION TIME 10 minutes, plus 4 hours chilling (optional), plus making the raita
COOKING TIME 12 to 16 minutes **SERVES** 4

olive oil, for frying and greasing
1 onion, finely chopped
1 lb. 2 oz. ground turkey
4 tbsp. tikka masala paste
3 tbsp. chopped cilantro

2 tbsp. plain yogurt
1 tbsp. mango chutney
salt and freshly ground black pepper
4 small naan breads and 1 recipe quantity
Raita (see page 38), to serve

1 Heat a little oil in a skillet, add the onion, and fry over medium heat until soft. Remove from
the heat and leave to cool.

2 Put all the remaining ingredients in a bowl and mix until thoroughly combined. With wet hands,
form the mixture into 4 link sausages. If possible, cover and leave in a cool place for 4 hours
or overnight, to let the flavors develop.

3 Preheat the broiler to medium. Cook the sausages on a greased broiler rack under the preheated
broiler 6 to 8 minutes on each side until the juices run clear, turning them carefully with
a pancake turner or metal spatula.

4 Remove the sausages from the broiler and warm the naan breads 20 to 30 seconds under the
broiler. Serve the sausages with the naan breads and raita.

052 Potatoes with Chorizo, Arugula & Tomatoes

PREPARATION TIME 5 minutes   COOKING TIME 20 minutes   SERVES 2 to 3

3 cups potatoes cut into ¾-in. chunks
scant 1 cup chopped chorizo
olive oil, for frying
9 oz. ripe well-flavored tomatoes, halved
    lengthwise

2 tsp. balsamic vinegar
2 tbsp. sun-dried tomato and
    olive tapenade
2 oz. arugula leaves
freshly ground black pepper

1 Cook the potatoes in a saucepan of boiling salted water about 10 minutes until just tender.

2 Meanwhile, fry the chorizo in a little olive oil in a nonstick skillet 2 to 3 minutes. Add the
   tomatoes and balsamic vinegar and cook until the tomatoes are just beginning to collapse.

3 Drain the potatoes and coarsely chop. Stir them into the skillet with the tapenade, then stir in
   the arugula and black pepper and serve.

053 Sausage & Mushroom Casserole

PREPARATION TIME 10 minutes   **COOKING TIME** 30 to 35 minutes   **SERVES** 4 to 6

1 lb. pork and herb link sausages
olive oil, for frying
1 onion, finely chopped
2 garlic cloves, finely chopped
3½ cups chopped mushrooms
1 tbsp. thyme leaves

2 cans (15-oz.) crushed tomatoes
1 to 2 cans (15-oz.) soy-, navy, or borlotti
  beans, drained and rinsed
salt and freshly ground black pepper
small handful flat-leaf parsley

1 Heat a little oil in a nonstick skillet and fry the sausages over medium heat, turning them
  frequently, until evenly brown. Transfer to a large saucepan. (If this dish is to serve 6 people,
  chop the sausages at this point.) Fry the onion and garlic, adding a little extra oil, if necessary,
  until evenly brown. Transfer to the pan.

2 Add the mushrooms and thyme to the skillet and cook until the liquid from the mushrooms
  evaporates, but do not let them become too dry. Season. Add to the pan with the tomatoes
  and beans (using 1 can to serve 4 or 2 cans to serve 6).

3 Bring to a boil, then lower the heat and simmer slowly, covered, 15 minutes. If there is too
  much liquid, remove the lid and simmer 5 to 10 minutes longer. (If using 2 cans of beans,
  leave the lid on throughout the cooking.) Scatter the parsley over the top and serve.

054 Pasta with Bacon, Tomatoes & Chili

PREPARATION TIME 10 minutes   **COOKING TIME** 30 minutes   **SERVES** 4

olive oil, for frying
1 onion, finely chopped
4 oz. smoked Canadian bacon,
  cut into strips
1 garlic clove, finely chopped
pinch of chili flakes, to taste

5 tbsp. dry white wine
2 cans (15-oz.) crushed plum tomatoes
14 oz. small pasta shapes
3 tbsp. freshly grated Parmesan cheese,
  plus extra to serve
salt and freshly ground black pepper

1 Heat a little oil in a large skillet and fry the onion and bacon over medium heat until the bacon is brown but not crisp, and the onion is soft and turning golden. Add the garlic and chili flakes toward the end of the cooking.

2 Pour in the wine and bring to a boil, then bubble until it evaporates by about three-quarters. Add the tomatoes and continue simmering until thick. Season to taste.

3 Meanwhile, cook the pasta in a large saucepan of boiling salted water following the package directions until just cooked, or al dente, then drain well. Toss with the sauce and the Parmesan and serve with additional Parmesan.

055 Potato, Chorizo & Mozzarella Tortilla

PREPARATION TIME 10 minutes   **COOKING TIME** 35 to 40 minutes   **SERVES** 4

1 lb. 2 oz. potatoes, halved

3 to 4 tbsp. olive oil

7 oz. mozzarella cheese, drained and very thinly sliced

8 to 12 basil leaves

3½ cups very thinly sliced chorizo

4 eggs, beaten

2 large red bell peppers, halved and seeded

salt and freshly ground black pepper

1 Cook the potatoes in a saucepan of boiling salted water about 10 minutes until just tender. Drain well, then, when cool enough to handle, slice thinly.

2 Preheat the broiler to high. Pour a little of the oil into a large, nonstick skillet, and place an even layer of half the potato slices on the bottom. Top with the mozzarella, basil leaves, chorizo, and then the remaining potato. Set aside.

3 Cook the peppers in a broiler pan under the preheated broiler 10 to 15 minutes until charred and blistered. Leave until cool enough to handle, then peel off the skins and slice the flesh.

4 Meanwhile, season the eggs, then pour them over the potatoes. Cook over medium heat about 8 minutes until the underneath is golden.

5 Put a large plate over the top. Flip the pan over so the tortilla falls onto the plate. Add a little more oil to the pan and slide the tortilla back in. Cook 5 to 6 minutes longer until the other side is golden. Flip out of the pan onto a warm serving plate. Serve in large wedges, accompanied by the broiled red peppers.

056 Sausage & Eggplant Lasagne

PREPARATION TIME 20 minutes, plus making the sauce   **COOKING TIME** 50 minutes   **SERVES** 6

12 lasagne sheets
olive oil, for cooking the lasagne,
   brushing and greasing
9 oz. link sausages
4¾ cups eggplant, cut into
   ¼-in. slices

¾ cup freshly grated Parmesan cheese
1 recipe quantity Béchamel Sauce
   (see page 90)
6 oz. mozzarella cheese, sliced
2 well-flavored tomatoes, sliced
salt and freshly ground black pepper

1 Preheat the broiler to high.

2 Cook the lasagne sheets in batches in boiling salted water, to which a little oil has been added, 3 minutes for fresh lasagne or 7 minutes for dried. Drain the lasagne, then rinse it and drain again. Spread on a clean dish towel to dry. (Follow these instructions even if you are using no-pre-cook lasagne.)

3 Meanwhile, grill the sausages on a greased broiler rack under the preheated grill until evenly brown. Drain well on paper towels, then slice thinly.

4 Lay the eggplant slices in a single layer on a large baking sheet (you might need to use two sheets), brush lightly with oil and season. Broil until tender and brown on both sides. Preheat the oven to 350°F.

5 Stir three-quarters of the Parmesan into the béchamel sauce, then spread a thin layer of the sauce over the bottom of a greased baking dish (about 10 x 6¼ x 3 inches). Cover with a layer of 3 lasagne sheets and arrange half the eggplant and sausage slices on top. Add another layer of sauce, one of lasagne and then half the mozzarella. Cover with half the tomatoes, another layer of lasagne sheets, the remaining eggplants and sausages, more sauce, remaining lasagne, and the rest of the mozzarella and tomatoes. Finish with a generous layer of cheese sauce. Sprinkle the remaining Parmesan over.

6 Bake in the preheated oven about 30 minutes until bubbling and brown, then serve.

057 Spaghetti alla Carbonara

PREPARATION TIME 5 minutes **COOKING TIME** 10 to 12 minutes **SERVES** 2 to 3

9 oz. spaghetti

small pat of unsalted butter

3 oz. smoked Canadian bacon,
cut into strips

4 tbsp. dry white wine

2 eggs

2 tbsp. finely chopped flat-leaf parsley

2 tbsp. freshly grated pecorino cheese

2 tbsp. freshly grated Parmesan cheese

salt and freshly ground black pepper

1 Cook the spaghetti in a large saucepan of boiling salted water following the package directions until just cooked, or al dente.

2 Meanwhile, melt the butter in a skillet and fry the bacon until crisp. Add the wine and boil until it reduces by half.

3 While the bacon is cooking, in a bowl that is large enough to hold the cooked pasta, beat the eggs with the parsley, half of each of the cheeses, a pinch of salt and plenty of black pepper.

4 Drain the pasta and immediately add it to the bowl of eggs. Quickly toss together, adding the bacon as well, until the eggs are creamy. Toss lightly with the remaining cheese and serve.

058 Ham with Paprika Spice Rub

PREPARATION TIME 15 minutes, plus 2 hours marinating   **COOKING TIME** 10 to 12 minutes   **SERVES** 4

4 boneless uncooked ham steaks, cut from
   the center of the shank, about 6 oz. each
2 tsp. ground cumin
2 tsp. paprika
4 tsp. dark brown sugar
4 tbsp. olive oil

MANGO SALSA
2 large ripe mangoes
juice of 2 limes
½ red onion, finely chopped
3 tbsp. finely chopped cilantro
pinch of dark soft brown sugar
salt and freshly ground black pepper

1 Trim any surplus fat from the ham steaks, leaving just enough to keep them moist. Snip the remaining fat at 1-inch intervals.

2 Mix the cumin, paprika, sugar, and oil together and rub all over the ham steaks. Cover and leave to marinate in a cool place 2 hours.

3 Meanwhile, preheat the broiler to high. Peel the mangoes, then cut the flesh away from the seed with a knife. Dice a quarter of the flesh. Puree the remaining flesh with the lime juice, then stir in the onion, cilantro, and diced mango. Add the sugar and seasoning to taste.

4 Cook the ham on a greased broiler rack under the preheated broiler 5 to 6 minutes on each side until the flesh is cooked through juices run clear when pierced with a fine skewer. Serve hot with the salsa.

059 Spanish Burgers

PREPARATION TIME 15 minutes, plus 4 to 8 hours marinating   COOKING TIME 15 minutes   SERVES 4

1 tbsp. olive oil
1 onion, finely chopped
1 lb. 2 oz. coarsely ground pork
½ cup finely chopped chorizo
3 tbsp. chopped oregano
all-purpose flour, for dusting
salt and freshly ground black pepper

MARINADE
scant ⅔ cup olive oil
2 garlic cloves, crushed
1 tbsp. sun-dried tomato paste
1 tbsp. chopped thyme
2 tsp. chopped parsley

TO SERVE
4 hamburger buns or rolls,
    split into halves
mayonnaise
lettuce
chopped tomatoes
scallions

1 Heat the oil in a skillet and fry the onion over medium heat until soft. Leave to cool, then mix with the pork, chorizo, oregano, and seasoning. With floured hands, form into 4 burgers, ¾ to 1 inch thick. Place in a single layer in a shallow dish.

2 Mix the marinade ingredients together in a pitcher. Pour over the burgers and turn them over so they are evenly coated, then cover and leave in a cool place 4 to 8 hours.

3 Lift the burgers from the marinade, reserving it. Cook the burgers in a preheated, greased griddle pan 6 minutes on each side, brushing occasionally with the marinade.

4 Meanwhile, toast the halved rolls. Serve the burgers in the rolls with the mayonnaise, lettuce, tomatoes, and scallions.

060 Bacon-Wrapped Sausages with Mustard Dip

PREPARATION TIME 10 minutes, plus 20 minutes soaking the toothpicks   **COOKING TIME** 12 to 14 minutes
SERVES 4 to 6

12 pork link sausages

12 smoked bacon slices

2 tbsp. thyme leaves (optional)

MUSTARD DIP

4 tbsp. wholegrain mustard

½ cup mayonnaise

1 Soak 12 wooden toothpicks 20 minutes. Drain and set aside. Preheat the broiler to medium-
  high.Make the mustard dip by beating the mustard into the mayonnaise.
2 Stretch each bacon slice with the back of a knife. Sprinkle the thyme, if using, over one side
  of each slice. Place a sausage diagonally across one end of each slice and roll up to enclose
  the sausage completely, securing the bacon with a toothpick.
3 Cook the wrapped sausages on a greased broiler rack under the preheated broiler about
  15 minutes until brown and cooked through, turning regularly. Serve hot with the dip.

061 Pork & Apple Skewers

PREPARATION TIME 10 minutes, plus 3 to 4 hours marinating   **COOKING TIME** 12 to 15 minutes
SERVES 4

1 lb. pork tenderloin, cut into 1¼-in. cubes
1 tbsp. finely chopped sage leaves
4 tbsp. sharp apple juice
juice and finely grated zest of ½ lemon
2 tbsp. wholegrain mustard

4 tbsp. grapeseed oil, plus extra for greasing
salt and freshly ground black pepper
2 crisp red apples
few sage sprigs

1 Put the pork into a nonmetallic bowl.
2 Mix the sage, apple juice, lemon juice and zest, mustard, oil, and salt and black pepper
   together in a pitcher. Stir into the pork so the cubes are evenly coated, then cover and leave
   to marinate in a cool place 3 to 4 hours.
3 Meanwhile, core the apples and cut into wedges. Preheat the broiler to medium-high.
4 Lift the pork from the bowl, reserving the marinade. Thread the pork and apple alternately
   onto skewers, interspersing the pieces with sage leaves.
5 Cook on a greased broiler rack under the preheated broiler 12 to 15 minutes, turning
   regularly and brushing with the remaining marinade, until the pork is cooked through.

062 Pork Chops with Plum Sauce

PREPARATION TIME 15 minutes **COOKING TIME** 30 to 35 minutes **SERVES** 6

6 pork chops, about 1 in. thick

peanut oil, for brushing

salt and freshly ground black pepper

PLUM SAUCE

1 tbsp. peanut oil

2 shallots, finely chopped

1 tbsp. finely chopped fresh gingerroot

1½ tsp. Sichuan peppercorns, finely crushed

8 oz. plums, quartered and pitted

1 tbsp. light soy sauce

5 tbsp. sweet sherry

1½ tsp. honey

lime juice, to taste

1 Make the plum sauce by heating the oil in a skillet, adding the shallots, and frying until soft. Add the ginger and peppercorns toward the end and continue cooking until they smell fragrant. Add the plums, soy sauce, sherry, and honey. Bring to a boil, then reduce the heat and simmer, covered, until the plums are tender. Add lime juice to taste. Set aside.

2 Preheat the oven to 400°F, or preheat the broiler to medium-high.

3 Trim any excess fat from the chops and snip the remaining fat at 1-inch intervals. Brush the chops with oil and season them. Place in a baking dish.

4 Cook the chops in the preheated oven about 25 minutes, or under the broiler 12 to 15 minutes, until the juices run clear when the thickest part is pierced with a skewer. Meanwhile, warm the sauce in a saucepan over low heat. Serve the chops with the sauce.

063 Char Sui Pork

PREPARATION TIME 10 minutes, plus 4 to 6 hours marinating   **COOKING TIME** 14 to 16 minutes
SERVES 4

4 bonless pork shoulder chops

MARINADE
1 tbsp. sunflower oil
1 tbsp. sesame oil
2 tbsp. hoisin sauce
2 tbsp. honey
2 tbsp. soy sauce
1 tsp. Chinese five-spice powder
freshly ground black pepper
2 garlic cloves, finely chopped
2-in. piece fresh gingerroot, grated

TO SERVE
6 scallions, sliced lengthwise into
   thin shreds
½ cucumber, seeded and cut into long,
   thin strips
Chinese plum sauce
lime wedges

1 Lay the pork steaks in a single layer in a shallow, nonmetallic dish.
2 Make the marinade by stirring together all the ingredients, except the ginger. Using a garlic
   press, squeeze the ginger juice into the other ingredients, then stir in. Pour over the pork, turn
   the chops so they are completely coated, then cover the dish and leave to marinate in a cool
   place 4 to 6 hours, turning occasionally. Preheat the broiler to medium-high.
3 Lift the pork from the marinade (reserving the remaining marinade) and cook on a greased
   broiler rack under the preheated broiler 14 to 16 minutes, turning once and basting with any
   remaining marinade, until the juices run clear when the thickest part of the chops is pierced
   with a skewer. Serve the steaks with the scallions, cucumber, plum sauce, and lime wedges.

064 Pizza with Eggplant & Chorizo

PREPARATION TIME 10 minutes, plus rising time and making the sauce
COOKING TIME 20 to 30 minutes   **SERVES** 4

2½ cups bread flour, plus extra for rolling
2 tsp. quick-acting active dry yeast
1 tsp. salt
scant 1 cup warm water
2 tbsp. olive oil, plus extra for brushing
1½ x recipe quantity Red Pepper & Tomato
   Sauce, omitting the basil (see page 54)
freshly ground black pepper

TOPPING
1 eggplant, sliced
olive oil, for greasing and brushing
1 cup chopped chorizo
¾ cup crumbled feta cheese
3 oz. mozzarella cheese, grated
small handful of fresh basil leaves, torn

1 Stir the flour, yeast, salt, and some pepper together in a bowl. Make a well in the middle and pour in the water and oil, bringing the flour mixture into the liquids to make a soft dough. Knead on a floured surface 10 to 15 minutes until firm and elastic.

2 Turn the dough over in a greased bowl, cover, and leave to rise until double in volume. Preheat the broiler to high.

3 Brush the eggplant slices with oil and broil until tender and lightly charred.

4 Preheat the oven to 425°F. Knock the dough back and divide it in half. Roll each piece out on a lightly floured surface into an even 10-inch circle. Transfer to two baking sheets.

5 Brush the tops of the pizzas with oil. Spread the pepper and tomato sauce over, leaving a ½-inch border. Arrange the eggplant slices over the top, then scatter with the chorizo and cheeses. Season with plenty of black pepper and scatter with the basil. Brush the tops of the pizzas again with oil.

6 Cook in the preheated oven 15 to 20 minutes until the cheese melts.

065 Sweet & Sticky Spareribs

PREPARATION TIME 5 minutes   **COOKING TIME** 1 hour   **SERVES** 6

5 garlic cloves, crushed and finely chopped

3-in. piece fresh gingerroot, grated

6 tbsp. soy sauce

6 tbsp. dry sherry

6 tbsp. honey

2 tsp. chili sauce

3 lb. meaty pork spareribs

lemon wedges, to serve

1 Preheat the oven to 400°F. Combine the garlic, ginger, soy sauce, sherry, honey, and chili sauce in a bowl to make the baste.

2 Lay the ribs in a large, foil-lined roasting pan, pour the baste over the top, and cook in the preheated oven 15 minutes, then lower the temperature to 325°F and cook 45 minutes longer.

3 Remove the pan from the oven and transfer to a board, then divide into individual ribs. Serve with the lemon wedges.

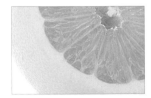

066 Cilantro–Noodle Salad

PREPARATION TIME 10 minutes   COOKING TIME 10 minutes   SERVES 4

1 lb. lean boneless pork, cubed

1 garlic clove, finely crushed

olive oil, for frying

8 oz. dried Chinese egg noodles

6 scallions, thinly sliced on the diagonal

1 tbsp. soy sauce

2 tbsp. Thai fish sauce

1½ tbsp. sesame oil

juice and finely grated zest of 1 lime

2 tbsp. peanut oil

2 tbsp. sesame seeds, lightly toasted

3 tbsp. chopped cilantro

2 tbsp. chopped fresh gingerroot

few drops of chili oil

freshly ground black pepper

1 Fry the pork and garlic in a little oil in a skillet over medium heat about 10 minutes, stirring frequently, until light brown and cooked through.

2 Meanwhile, cook the noodles in a saucepan of boiling water following the package directions. While the pork is cooking, combine the remaining ingredients in a bowl or pitcher.

3 Drain the noodles into a colander, then tip into a serving bowl with the pork and garlic. Pour the dressing over and toss well to mix.

067 Koftas

PREPARATION TIME 15 minutes, plus at least 4 hours marinating and making the raita
COOKING TIME 10 to 13 minutes   SERVES 4

1 small onion, quartered
2 garlic cloves, chopped
1-in. piece fresh gingerroot, chopped
1 tsp. ground cumin
1 tsp. ground coriander
1 tbsp. olive oil, plus extra for brushing
1 lb. frozen ground lamb, thawed

3 tbsp. chopped cilantro
1 egg, beaten
salt and freshly ground black pepper
cumin seeds, toasted and crushed,
    for sprinkling
1 recipe quantity Raita (see page 38)
    and some lemon wedges, to serve

1 Put the onion, garlic, and ginger in a small blender or food processor and blend until finely chopped. Add the spices and mix again until evenly combined.

2 Heat the oil in a skillet, add the onion mixture, and fry 2 to 3 minutes, stirring. Leave to cool.

3 Put the lamb into a bowl and break it up with a fork. Add the cold onion mixture, the cilantro, and seasoning, then mix in enough egg to bind, but don't add so much that the mixture becomes sticky. Cover and keep in a cool place up to 4 hours, or overnight, if possible, in the refrigerator.

4 Preheat the broiler to high. Divide the mixture into 8 equal portions. With wet hands, mold each portion into a long sausage shape around a skewer (soaked if wooden).

5 Brush the koftas with oil and cook on a greased broiler rack under the preheated broiler 8 to 10 minutes, turning occasionally, until nicely brown on the outside and cooked to your liking inside.

6 Sprinkle the koftas with the cumin seeds and serve with the raita and lemon wedges.

068 Butterflied Chinese Lamb

PREPARATION TIME 15 minutes, plus at least 8 hours marinating **COOKING TIME** 1 hour 5 to 10 minutes
SERVES 8

1 butterflied shoulder of lamb,
    about 2 lb. 7 oz.
4 garlic cloves, cut into thin slivers

MARINADE
⅔ cup soy sauce
⅔ cup medium-dry sherry
1-in. piece fresh gingerroot, grated
1 tbsp. honey
3 star anise
3 tbsp. chopped cilantro
freshly ground black pepper

1 Make the marinade by mixing all the ingredients in a blender.
2 Open out the lamb and cut a few slits all over the surface. Insert the garlic slivers into the slits.
    Put the lamb into a baking dish and pour the marinade over. Cover and leave in a cool place
    8 hours or overnight, turning occasionally. Preheat the oven to 400°F.
3 Lift the lamb from the marinade (reserving the marinade), transfer to a roasting pan, and cook in
    the preheated oven 1 hour 5 to 10 minutes, basting occasionally with the remaining marinade.
    Remove from the oven, cover the pan with foil, and leave to rest 10 minutes before carving.

069 Baked Rigatoni alla Bolognese

PREPARATION TIME 5 minutes, plus making the sauce and ragu   COOKING TIME 25 to 30 minutes
SERVES 4 to 6

1 lb. rigatoni

6 tbsp. freshly grated Parmesan cheese

⅔ recipe quantity Béchamel Sauce
   (see page 90)

olive oil, for drizzling

FOR THE RAGU

1 large onion, finely chopped

1 carrot, finely chopped

1 small celery stick, finely chopped

olive oil, for frying

2 garlic cloves, finely chopped

1 lb. ground beef

1⅓ cups dry red wine

1⅓ cups beef stock

1 can (15-oz.) crushed tomatoes

1 tbsp. sun-dried tomato paste

2 tsp. dried oregano

salt and freshly ground black pepper

1 Preheat the oven to 400°F.

2 To make the ragu sauce, fry the onion, carrot, and celery in a little oil in a heavy-bottomed pan until soft. Add the garlic and cook 1 minute, then stir in the beef and cook, stirring, until light brown. Stir in the remaining ingredients and bring to a boil, then lower the heat and simmer, half-covered, stirring occasionally, about 40 minutes until the sauce reduces.

3 Cook the rigatoni in a large saucepan of boiling water following the package directions, but 2 minutes less than suggested, then drain well. Toss the pasta with 4 tablespoons of the Parmesan, then add the ragu and béchamel sauce. When well mixed, spread evenly in a gratin dish, sprinkle the remaining Parmesan over and drizzle with a little oil.

4 Bake 15 to 20 minutes until brown. Leave to stand 5 minutes before serving.

070 Lasagne alla Bolognese

PREPARATION TIME 15 minutes, plus making the ragu and 30 minutes infusing
COOKING TIME 45 minutes   **SERVES** 6

12 lasagne sheets
olive oil, for cooking the pasta and greasing
1 recipe quantity Ragu (see page 88)
3 tbsp. freshly grated Parmesan cheese

BÉCHAMEL SAUCE
3 cups milk
1 bay leaf
1 onion slice
1 clove
5 tbsp. butter
6 tbsp. all-purpose flour

1 Preheat the oven to 400ºF.

2 Cook the lasagne sheets in batches in boiling salted water, to which a little oil has been added, 3 minutes for fresh lasagne or 7 minutes for dried. Drain the lasagne, then rinse it and drain again. Spread on a clean dish towel to dry. (Follow these directions even if using no-pre-cook lasagne.)

3 To make the béchamel sauce, gently heat the milk with the bay leaf, onion slice, and clove, then remove from the heat, cover, and leave to infuse 30 minutes. Melt the butter over low heat in a heavy-bottomed saucepan, then stir in the flour and mix to a paste. Cook 1 to 2 minutes. Remove the pan from the heat and slowly strain in the milk, whisking or stirring continually to prevent lumps forming. Once all the milk has been incorporated, return the pan to the heat and just bring to a boil, then simmer 5 minutes, stirring occasionally. Season.

4 Using a large spoon, spread a thin layer of béchamel over the bottom of a greased baking dish (about 12 x 8 x 3 inches). Add a layer of 4 lasagne sheets, then one of ragu. Add another layer of béchamel sauce, followed by a layer of lasagne. Repeat the layering to make 3 layers of pasta, 3 of ragu, and 4 of béchamel. Sprinkle the Parmesan over the top layer of béchamel.

5 Bake in the preheated oven about 25 minutes until the top is crisp and golden and the lasagne heated throughout. Leave to stand for 5 minutes before serving.

071 Beef & Mushroom Burgers

PREPARATION TIME 15 minutes, plus 20 minutes soaking   **COOKING TIME** 13 to 15 minutes   **SERVES** 4

2 tbsp. dried mushrooms
small pat of unsalted butter
2 cups chopped mushrooms
1 garlic clove, finely chopped
1 lb. ground beef
4 tsp. wholegrain mustard
2 tbsp. chopped herbs, such as marjoram,
   tarragon, parsley, sage, or thyme
salt and freshly ground black pepper

4 hamburger buns or rolls, split horizontally,
   and salad leaves, to serve

ROASTED RED PEPPER DRESSING
1 red bell pepper, halved and seeded
2 tbsp. balsamic vinegar
1 tsp. thyme
1 tsp. chopped garlic
6 tbsp. olive oil

1 Place the dried mushrooms in a heatproof bowl and just cover with boiling water. Leave to soak 20 minutes, then drain, pat dry, and chop finely.

2 Melt the butter in a skillet, add the fresh mushrooms and garlic, and fry until the liquid from the mushrooms is given off and they are tender. Stir in the soaked mushrooms just before the end of cooking. Leave to cool.

3 Mix the beef with the mushroom mixture, mustard, herbs, and seasoning until thoroughly combined. Divide the mixture into 4 equal portions. With wet hands, form each portion into a burger approximately 1 inch thick.

4 To make the dressing, grill the red pepper and remove the skin (see page 83). Put into a blender with the vinegar, thyme, and garlic. Pulse to mix, then, with the motor running, slowly pour in the olive oil until smooth. Season to taste.

5 Cook the burgers in a preheated, greased griddle pan 4 to 5 minutes on each side for medium-rare, or for longer if you prefer them more well done, turning them carefully.

6 Toast the rolls. Mix the salad leaves with a little dressing, then put them on the bottom of each roll. Top with the burgers and spoon a little dressing over. Cover with the tops of the rolls and serve.

Chapter 4

VEGETARIAN

Dishes that do not contain meat, poultry, or fish are often cheaper than those that do, but that does not mean that eating vegetarian meals is less fun or interesting; in fact, I think the opposite is true.

To keep costs down, buy dried beans and lentils rather than canned. The varieties on sale now cook more quickly than their cousins of yesteryear, with even chickpeas cooking in about 1 hour. Soaking cuts down the cooking time (to speed the soaking, boil the beans for 10 minutes, cover, and then leave to soak for just a couple of hours, or longer if you wish).

Cheese is used frequently in vegetarian cooking. Buy a sharp cheese with a good flavor, rather than a perhaps less-expensive mild one, otherwise you'll just use more. And make the most of herbs and spices for extra flavor to create stunning meals.

Gnocchi alla Romana (see page 94)

072 Gnocchi alla Romana

PREPARATION TIME 5 minutes, plus 2 hours chilling   **COOKING TIME** 25 to 30 minutes   **SERVES** 4

2 cloves

2 onions

4¼ cups milk

2 bay leaves

1 cup semolina

2 egg yolks

¾ cup freshly grated Parmesan cheese

1 stick unsalted butter, melted, plus extra
   for greasing the gratin dish

1 tbsp. Dijon mustard

salt and freshly ground black pepper

crisp green salad, to serve

1 Stick the cloves into the onions. Pour the milk into a heavy-bottomed saucepan and add the onions and bay leaves. Bring to a boil slowly, then remove the pan from the heat, cover, and leave to infuse 10 minutes. Strain the milk and return to the rinsed-out pan. Bring to a boil, then lower the heat to medium and gradually whisk in the semolina in a thin, steady stream. Return to a boil, reduce the heat, and simmer 3 to 5 minutes, until thick and smooth, stirring.

2 Off the heat, gradually beat in the egg yolks, then add two-thirds of the Parmesan, half the butter, and the mustard. Season, using plenty of black pepper. Using a dampened metal spatula or back of a spoon, spread the mixture in a layer about ½ inch thick on a moist baking sheet. Brush with the remaining butter. Leave to cook and then chill about 2 hours, until firm.

3 Meanwhile, preheat the oven to 450°F.

4 Cut the gnocchi into 2-inch circles with a plain cookie cutter. Arrange in a buttered gratin dish or individual dishes and sprinkle with the remaining Parmesan. Bake in the preheated oven 15 to 20 minutes, until hot and brown. Serve accompanied by a crisp green salad.

073 Tagliatelle with Green Beans & Herbs

PREPARATION TIME 10 minutes **COOKING TIME** 15 minutes **SERVES** 4

2 cups mixed frozen runner beans,
  green beans, and peas
14 oz. tagliatelle
1 garlic clove, crushed
olive oil, for frying
5 oz. soft, mild goat cheese, chopped
small bunch of flat-leaf parsley,
  finely chopped

leaves from a small bunch of young mint,
  finely chopped
7 tbsp. crème fraîche
salt and freshly ground black pepper
2 tbsp. lightly toasted pine nuts and some
  shaved pecorino cheese, to serve

1 Bring a large saucepan of water to a boil, add the beans and peas, and cook 3 to 4 minutes until almost tender. Remove with a slotted spoon and set aside. Bring the water back to a boil, add the pasta to the pan, and cook according to the package directions until just cooked, or al dente.

2 Meanwhile, fry the garlic in a little oil in a skillet over low heat about 2 minutes. Add the goat cheese, herbs, and crème fraîche. Slice the runner beans thinly lengthways and the green beans in half widthways and add to the mixture. Warm through and season.

3 Drain the pasta and toss with the sauce. Serve scattered with the pine nuts and pecorino.

074 Pasta with Zucchinis, Lemon & Pine Nuts

PREPARATION TIME 10 minutes   **COOKING TIME** 10 minutes   **SERVES** 4

2 cups pasta shapes, such as torchieti
  or fusilli

2 large garlic cloves, thinly sliced

4 tbsp. virgin olive oil

1 lb. 4 oz. small zucchini, pared into
  ribbons using a vegetable peeler

juice and finely grated zest of 1 large lemon

6 tbsp. heavy cream

2 tbsp. finely chopped flat-leaf parsley

5 tbsp. pine nuts, lightly toasted

salt and freshly ground black pepper

freshly grated Parmesan cheese, to sprinkle

1 Cook the pasta in a large saucepan of boiling salted water following the package directions
until just cooked or al dente.

2 Meanwhile, put the garlic and oil in a small saucepan and warm 5 minutes. Do not let the
oil boil or the garlic will fry. Discard the garlic.

3 Pour the garlic-infused oil into a skillet and fry the zucchini briskly, in batches, until golden.
Return all the zucchini to the pan with the lemon juice and zest and the cream. Leave to
bubble 2 to 3 minutes, until slightly thicker, then season.

4 Drain the pasta, add to the zucchini sauce with the parsley and pine nuts, and toss together.
Sprinkle with Parmesan before serving.

075 Pappardelle with Squash & Goat Cheese

PREPARATION TIME 10 minutes   **COOKING TIME** 30 minutes   **SERVES** 4

1 small butternut squash, peeled, seeded,
   and cut into 1-in. chunks
several thyme sprigs
2 garlic cloves, crushed
3 tbsp. olive oil
10 oz. pappardelle

4 slices goat cheese
4 tbsp. finely chopped flat-leaf parsley
finely grated zest of ½ lemon
extra-virgin olive oil, to drizzle
freshly grated Parmesan cheese, to scatter
salt and freshly ground black pepper

1 Preheat the oven to 400°F.

2 Put the squash into a large roasting pan. Add the thyme, garlic, and oil and stir together to coat
   the squash. Roast in the preheated oven 25 to 30 minutes, until the squash is tender and
   tinged with brown. Discard the thyme.

3 Meanwhile, cook the pasta in a large saucepan of boiling water following the package directions
   until just cooked, or al dente, then drain well, reserving ½ cup of the cooking water.

4 Lay the goat cheese slices on a piece of lightly greased foil and broil 3 to 4 minutes until light
   brown and soft.

5 Toss the pasta with the squash and any pan juices, the parsley, lemon zest, and seasoning,
   adding enough of the reserved cooking water to moisten. Drizzle with extra-virgin olive oil and
   scatter with Parmesan, then place the goat cheese on top and serve.

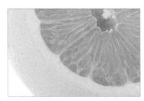

076 Risotto with Minted Lettuce & Peas

PREPARATION TIME 5 minutes   **COOKING TIME** 30 minutes   **SERVES** 4

1 onion, finely chopped

3 tbsp. unsalted butter

1½ cups risotto rice

⅔ cup medium-bodied dry white wine

3¾ cups boiling vegetable stock

1½ cups frozen peas

3 cups shredded crisp lettuce

2 tbsp. chopped mint

4 tbsp. crème fraîche (optional)

squeeze of lemon juice (optional)

salt and freshly ground black pepper

Fry the onion in the butter in a large skillet over medium heat until soft. Add the rice and stir
2 to 3 minutes until all the grains are coated with butter.

Add the wine and cook slowly, stirring occasionally, until the rice absorbes almost all the liquid,
then add the hot stock, a ladleful at a time, in the same way until the rice is thick and creamy
and just tender. Add the peas 5 minutes before the end of the cooking time.

Stir in the lettuce, mint and seasoning. Serve the risotto with a spoonful of crème fraîche stirred
into each portion or add a squeeze of lemon juice.

  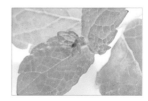

077 Pearl Barley with Mushrooms & Leeks

PREPARATION TIME 5 minutes   **COOKING TIME** 45 minutes   **SERVES** 4

olive oil, for frying
1½ cups sliced shiitake mushrooms
3 cups sliced cremini mushroom
2 leeks, sliced
3 garlic cloves, crushed
heaped 1 cup pearl barley

5 cups vegetable stock
leaves from a small bunch of flat-leaf
  parsley, finely chopped
salt and freshly ground black pepper
freshly grated Parmesan cheese,
  to sprinkle (optional)

1 Heat the oil in a large skillet and fry both types of mushrooms and the leeks over medium
  heat until golden, adding the garlic and pearl barley toward the end.
2 Add the vegetable stock and bring to a boil, then lower the heat and simmer, half-covered,
  about 40 minutes, until the barley is tender and all the liquid is absorbed (adding a little extra
  stock or some water, if necessary). Season and add the parsley. Sprinkle with Parmesan,
  if desired, and serve.

078 Spinach & Cheese Lasagne

PREPARATION TIME 15 minutes, plus making the sauce   **COOKING TIME** 45 minutes   **SERVES** 6

12 lasagne sheets

olive oil, for cooking the lasagne and oiling

2 lb. spinach, rinsed

small pat of unsalted butter

1 cup ricotta cheese

1½ cups crumbled gorgonzola cheese

1 recipe quantity Béchamel Sauce
 (see page 90)

4 tbsp. pine nuts, lightly toasted

½ cup freshly grated Parmesan cheese

7 oz. buffalo mozzarella cheese, grated

salt and freshly ground black pepper

Cook the lasagne sheets in batches in boiling salted water, to which a little oil has been added, 3 minutes for fresh lasagne or 7 minutes for dried. Drain the lasagne, then rinse it and drain again. Spread on a dish towel to dry. (Follow these directions even if using no-pre-cook lasagne.)

Preheat the oven to 350°F.

Cook the spinach in a large saucepan, with just the water clinging to its leaves, stirring frequently, until it wilts and is soft. Drain, chop coarsely, and then squeeze out as much water as possible. Combine with the butter, ricotta, gorgonzola, and seasoning.

Barely cover the base of a greased baking dish (about 10 x 6¼ x 3 inches) with some of the béchamel sauce. Cover with 3 of the lasagne sheets, then a quarter of the spinach mixture and scatter 1 tablespoon of the pine nuts over. Pour one-third of the remaining béchamel over and sprinkle a quarter of the Parmesan on top. Repeat the layers, adding a third of the mozzarella with the pine nuts, until the ingredients are used up, ending with mozzarella and Parmesan.

Bake in the preheated oven 30 to 35 minutes until bubbling and golden. Leave to stand 5 minutes before serving.

079 Zucchini & Ricotta Cannelloni

PREPARATION TIME 15 minutes, plus making the sauce   **COOKING TIME** 25 minutes   **SERVES** 4

12 lasagne verde sheets

olive oil, for cooking the lasagne, frying, and oiling

1 onion, chopped

4 zucchini, grated

2 garlic cloves, crushed and finely chopped

finely grated zest of 1 lemon

1 cup + 2 tbsp. ricotta cheese

salt and freshly ground black pepper

1 recipe quantity Red Pepper & Tomato Sauce (see page 54)

½ cup freshly grated Parmesan cheese

1 Cook the lasagne sheets in batches in boiling salted water, to which a little oil has been added, 3 minutes for fresh lasagne or 7 minutes for dried. Drain the lasagne, then rinse it and drain again. Spread on a dish towel to dry. (Follow these directions even if using no-pre-cook lasagne.)

2 Preheat the oven to 400°F.

3 Fry the onion in a little oil until soft but not colored. Stir in the zucchini and garlic and continue cooking, stirring frequently, until soft. Remove from the heat and add the lemon zest, half the ricotta, and some seasoning.

4 Spread the zucchini mixture down the middle of each lasagne sheet. Roll into tubes.

5 Pour half the sauce into an oiled large, shallow baking dish. Place the tubes on top, seam-side down. Pour the remaining sauce over, dot with the remaining ricotta, and sprinkle with Parmesan.

6 Bake in the preheated oven 15 minutes until golden. Leave to stand 5 minutes before serving.

080 Souffléed Macaroni Cheese

PREPARATION TIME 10 minutes **COOKING TIME** 25 to 30 minutes **SERVES** 4

2 cups macaroni

4 tbsp. unsalted butter

1 leek, finely chopped

½ cup + 1 tbsp. all-purpose flour

2½ cups milk

1 bay leaf, torn across

¾ cup ricotta cheese

1 cup grated Fontina cheese

1 cup freshly grated Parmesan cheese

4 eggs, separated

salt and freshly ground black pepper

1 Preheat the oven to 375°F.

2 Cook the macaroni in a large saucepan of boiling salted water following the package directions, but 1 minute less than suggested, then drain well.

3 Meanwhile, melt the butter in a heavy-bottomed saucepan and fry the leek over medium heat until soft, then stir in the flour and cook 1 minute. Gradually add the milk and bay leaf, stirring, and bring to a boil. Lower the heat and simmer 5 minutes, stirring occasionally. Discard the bay loaf. Off the heat, stir in the ricotta, Fontina, half the Parmesan, the egg yolks, and macaroni. Season.

4 Whisk the egg whites until soft peaks form. Stir a few spoonfuls into the sauce, then carefully fold in the remainder in 3 batches, using a large metal spoon.

5 Transfer the mixture into a large, shallow baking dish, scatter the remaining Parmesan over, and bake in the preheated oven 15 to 20 minutes until puffed, golden, and just set in the middle.

081 Mediterranean Vegetable Tart

PREPARATION TIME 25 minutes, plus at least 30 minutes chilling **COOKING TIME** 50 to 55 minutes
SERVES 4

1 eggplant, about 10 oz., sliced
olive oil, for frying
2½ cups sliced mushrooms
1 large red bell pepper, thinly sliced
1 onion, thinly sliced
4 large plum tomatoes, chopped
2 garlic cloves, chopped

1½ tbsp. chopped oregano
salt and freshly ground black pepper

PASTRY DOUGH
1⅔ cups all-purpose flour, plus extra
  for dusting
1 stick chilled butter, diced

1 To make the pastry dough , sift the flour and a little salt and pepper into a mixing bowl. Add the
  butter and rub it into the flour with your fingertips until the mixture resembles bread crumbs.
  Sprinkle 3 to 4 tablespoons iced water over, then quickly and lightly, using a round-bladed knife,
  stir the ingredients together until they form large lumps. With one hand, quickly bring the dough
  into a ball. Knead lightly and briefly, then wrap in plastic wrap and chill at least 30 minutes.
2 Meanwhile, stir-fry the eggplant in a little oil in a large, deep skillet until brown. Remove with
  a slotted spoon and drain on paper towels.
3 Add the mushrooms to the pan and fry until slightly soft, then remove with a slotted spoon.
  Repeat with the pepper. Fry the onion until light brown. Return the cooked vegetables to the
  pan, stir in the tomatoes, garlic, oregano, and seasoning and cook 15 minutes, stirring
  occasionally, until tender and thick. Preheat the oven to 400°F.
4 Meanwhile, roll out the dough on a floured work surface into a circle large enough to line a deep
  10¾-inch tart pan. Lift the dough into the pan. Prick the base, cover with waxed paper, and fill
  with baking beans, then bake 15 minutes. Remove the baking beans and paper and bake
  5 minutes longer until light brown and baked through. Fill the tart with the vegetable mixture
  and return to the oven 5 minutes to heat through, then serve. Alternatively, serve cold.

082 Vegetable Satay

PREPARATION TIME 15 minutes   **COOKING TIME** 20 minutes   **SERVES** 4

1 small squash, peeled and cut into chunks
2 leeks, cut into chunks
1 zucchini, cut into chunks
1½ cups halved mushrooms
3 tbsp. dark soy sauce
2 tsp. sesame oil
8 to 12 bay leaves

SATAY SAUCE
1 tbsp. peanut oil
1 shallot, finely chopped
2 garlic cloves, crushed
1 in. piece fresh gingerroot, grated
1 lemongrass stalk
1 red chili, seeded and finely chopped
1 tsp. curry powder
heaped ½ cup crunchy peanut butter
3 tbsp. chopped cilantro
a little sugar
salt and freshly ground black pepper

1 To make the sauce, heat the oil and fry the shallot, garlic, ginger, and lemongrass until soft. Stir in the chili and curry powder a couple of minutes, then stir in the peanut butter and 1 cup plus 2 tablespoons boiling water. Bring to a boil, add the cilantro, and season with a little sugar and salt and pepper to taste. Remove from the heat.

2 Meanwhile, preheat the broiler to high. Cook the squash in a pan of boiling water 5 minutes. Add the leeks and cook 3 minutes longer. Drain and cool under running cold water. Put into a bowl with the zucchini and mushrooms.

3 Combine the soy sauce, sesame oil, and some black pepper. Trickle over the vegetables and stir gently to coat all the vegetables.

4 Thread the vegetables alternately onto skewers, adding bay leaves along the way. Cook on a greased broiler rack under the preheated broiler about 8 minutes, turning occasionally.

5 Warm the satay sauce through and serve with the vegetables.

083 **Feta-Stuffed Onions**

PREPARATION TIME 15 minutes   COOKING TIME 35 minutes   SERVES 4

4 large onions, about 10 oz. each
small pat of unsalted butter
1 large leek, chopped
leaves from 4 thyme sprigs
2 tbsp. chopped parsley
1 cup crumbled feta cheese

8 sun-dried tomato halves in oil,
   drained and sliced
6 oil-cured black olives, pitted and chopped
2 egg yolks
freshly ground black pepper

1 Trim the root ends of the onions, but do not cut them off completely because they hold the layers together. Cut each onion in half from top to bottom. Remove the inner layers of each onion half, leaving a shell 2 layers thick. Chop the removed layers.

2 Add the onion shells to a saucepan of boiling water. Lower the heat and simmer 10 minutes. Lift the onions from the water with a slotted spoon and leave upside-down to drain. Preheat the oven to 350°F.

3 Meanwhile, melt the butter in a heavy-bottomed skillet. Add the chopped onion and cook over very low heat until very soft and golden. Add the leek about three-quarters of the way through. Stir in the thyme and parsley and leave to cool slightly, then add the feta, sun-dried tomatoes, olives, and egg yolks. Season with plenty of black pepper.

4 Place each onion shell upright in a greased baking dish and pile the filling into the shells. Cover with foil, then bake in the preheated oven 25 minutes. Serve hot.

084 Roasted Vegetables

PREPARATION TIME 15 minutes, plus 2 hours marinating   **COOKING TIME** 65 minutes   **SERVES** 4

2 lb. mixed vegetables, such as carrots,
 parsnips, zucchini, eggplant, endive,
 fennel bulb, red onion, small leeks
8 garlic cloves
4 rosemary sprigs
5 tbsp. virgin olive oil
1½ tsp. balsamic vinegar
salt and freshly ground black pepper

MUSTARD & CAPER SAUCE
¾ cup mayonnaise
1½ tsp. Dijon mustard
1½ tsp. capers, drained and chopped
3 tbsp. chopped flat-leaf parsley

1 Blanch the carrots and parsnips separately in boiling water 5 minutes, then drain and dry well.
2 Slice the zucchini and eggplant diagonally. Quarter the endive lengthwise and remove the core, but leave the leaves attached. Cut the fennel lengthwise into wedges. Cut the red onion into wedges, leaving them attached at the root end, and halve the leeks lengthways.
3 Place all the vegetables and the garlic in a large roasting pan and add the rosemary, olive oil, balsamic vinegar, and seasoning. Stir everything together, then cover with foil, and leave to marinate in a cool place 2 hours. Preheat the oven to 400°F.
4 Meanwhile, make the sauce by stirring the ingredients together. Set aside.
5 Cook the vegetables in the preheated oven 30 minutes, then remove the foil and cook 30 minutes longer, stirring occasionally, until they are tender and lightly charred. Remove from the oven and serve with the sauce.

085 Vegetable Fajitas

PREPARATION TIME 10 minutes, plus 4 hours marinating **COOKING TIME** 30 minutes **SERVES** 8

2 red and 2 yellow bell peppers, quartered

3 zucchini, sliced diagonally

2 eggplant, sliced diagonally

6 oz. baby corn cobs, halved lengthwise

3 mild red chilies

6 tbsp. olive oil

2 tbsp. chopped mixed parsley, oregano, and thyme

juice of 1 lime

freshly ground black pepper

16 soft flour tortillas

sour cream, cilantro sprigs, and lime wedges, to serve

AVOCADO & TOMATO RELISH

1 large avocado, seeded and finely chopped

3 tbsp. lime juice

½ red chili, pitted and finely chopped

1 vine-ripened plum tomato, seeded and diced

½ red onion, finely diced

handful cilantro leaves, chopped

1 Put all the vegetables, including the chilies, into a large bowl. Mix together the olive oil, herbs, lime juice, and black pepper to taste and stir into the vegetables, then cover the bowl and leave to marinate about 4 hours, stirring occasionally.

2 Meanwhile, make the relish by tossing the ingredients together. Cover and chill 30 minutes.

3 Lift the vegetables from the marinade and cook in batches in a preheated greased griddle pan until soft and lightly charred. Remove the vegetables that are cooked first as soon as they are ready, put into a bowl, and cover with plastic wrap.

4 Meanwhile, warm the tortillas following the package directions.

5 When the chilies are cool enough to handle, cut off the tops. Chop them, discarding the seeds.

6 Divide the vegetables and chilies among the tortillas. Top with avocado relish, spoon over the sour cream, and fold over. Serve with cilantro sprigs and lime wedges.

086 Spiced Lentil Patties

PREPARATION TIME 15 minutes, plus making the relish and at least 1 hour chilling
COOKING TIME 40 minutes to 1 hour   **SERVES** 4

heaped 1 cup green or brown lentils
3 tbsp. olive oil
2 large onions, finely chopped
2 carrots, finely chopped
1 celery stick, finely chopped
2 garlic cloves, finely chopped
1 tsp. ground cumin
1 tsp. ground coriander

3 tbsp. chopped parsley
3 tbsp. chopped cilantro
1 tbsp. lemon juice
salt and freshly ground black pepper
seasoned all-purpose flour, for coating
1 recipe quantity Yogurt & Mint Relish
   (see page 111)

1 Cook the lentils in boiling unsalted water 20 to 30 minutes until tender. Drain well and leave
   to cool.

2 Meanwhile, heat 1 tablespoon of the olive oil in a large skillet and fry the onions, carrots, and
   celery over medium heat 10 minutes until soft and light brown. Stir in the lentils, garlic, spices,
   herbs, lemon juice, and seasoning. Scrape into a food processor or blender and blend
   to a coarse puree that holds together. Alternatively, mash with a potato masher.

3 With floured hands, form the mixture into 12 burgers, each ½ to ¾ inch thick. Coat the burgers
   in seasoned flour and pat in gently. Cover and chill at least 1 hour to firm up, or overnight,
   if possible, to allow the flavors to develop.

4 Heat 1 tablespoon of the oil in the skillet and cook the burgers in batches 5 to 7 minutes on
   each side until crisp and brown. Remove with a fish slice and leave each batch to drain on
   paper towels in a warm place while you cook the remaining burgers in the remaining oil. Serve
   with the avocado and tomato relish.

087 Falafel Burgers with Yogurt & Mint Relish

PREPARATION TIME 10 minutes, plus 2 hours chilling   **COOKING TIME** 10 to 20 minutes   **SERVES** 4

2 cans (15-oz.) chickpeas,
　　drained and rinsed
1 garlic clove, chopped
2 tbsp. tahini
1 tsp. ground cumin
1 tsp. ground coriander
1 cup fresh bread crumbs
3 tbsp. chopped cilantro
seasoned all-purpose flour, for dusting
olive oil, for greasing
salt and freshly ground black pepper
pita bread and lettuce leaves, to serve

YOGURT & MINT RELISH
1 small garlic clove, peeled
⅔ cup Greek yogurt
4 tbsp. chopped mint, plus small sprigs
　　of mint leaves, to garnish
dash of hot-pepper sauce

1 Put all the burger ingredients, except the flour, into a food processor and mix until the
chickpeas are finely chopped, but do not let the mixture turn into a puree.
2 Transfer to a bowl and stir in about 2 tablespoons of water, kneading until the mixture holds
together. With well-floured hands, form the mixture into 8 burgers, each about 1 inch thick.
Chill at least 2 hours. Preheat the broiler to high.
3 To make the relish, crush the garlic with a pinch of salt, then mix it with the yogurt. Add
the mint and season with hot-pepper sauce and black pepper to taste. Chill before serving.
Garnish with the mint leaves to serve.
4 Cook the burgers on a greased broiler rack under the preheated broiler about 5 minutes on each
side (in batches, if necessary) until crisp and brown on the outside and warm throughout.
5 Meanwhile, warm the pita breads in a microwave oven or toaster. Split the pita breads open,
add the falafel, and top with the lettuce. Serve with the yogurt and mint relish.

088 Leek & Goat Cheese Sausages

PREPARATION TIME 20 minutes, plus 4½ hours chilling   **COOKING TIME** 20 to 25 minutes   **SERVES** 4

2 cups potatoes cut into small chunks
3 oz. soft goat cheese
1 tbsp. butter, plus extra for greasing
1 cup finely chopped leeks
½ cup crumbled feta cheese
½ cup fresh bread crumbs, plus extra
  for coating
salt and freshly ground black pepper
1 to 2 eggs (as needed), beaten
salad leaves and mayonnaise, to serve

1 Cook the potatoes in boiling salted water 10 to 15 minutes until tender, then drain well. Return
  to the pan over low heat and shake the pan gently to dry the potatoes. Remove from the heat.
  Mash the potatoes and beat in the goat cheese. Set aside.
2 Melt the butter in a skillet and fry the leeks over low heat until very soft and dry. Beat them into
  the potatoes with the feta, bread crumbs, and seasoning, using plenty of black pepper. Transfer
  to a plate, cover, and chill for at least 4 hours.
3 With floured hands, shape the mixture into 8 link sausages. Put the beaten egg(s) in a bowl and
  the extra bread crumbs on a plate. Dip the sausages in the beaten egg, then roll them in the
  bread crumbs until they are evenly coated, pressing the crumbs in lightly. Cover with plastic
  wrap and chill 30 minutes. Preheat the broiler to high.
4 Cook on greased broiler rack under the preheated broiler about 3 minutes until brown and crisp,
  then turn over and cook on the other side. Serve with a green salad and mayonnaise, if desired.

089 Zucchini Burgers with Dill Tzatziki

PREPARATION TIME 15 minutes, plus 1½ to 2 hours degorging and chilling
COOKING TIME 15 to 20 minutes   **SERVES** 4

4 cups grated zucchini
3 cups fresh bread crumbs
2 eggs, lightly beaten
6 scallions, very finely chopped
heaped 1 tbsp. chopped mint
heaped 2 tbsp. chopped parsley
all-purpose flour, for dusting

salt and freshly ground black pepper
olive oil, for frying
4 ciabatta rolls, split into halves

DILL TZATZIKI
1⅔ cups Greek yogurt
2 tbsp. chopped dill

1 Layer the zucchini and a good sprinkling of salt in a colander. Leave 30 to 60 minutes.

2 Meanwhile, preheat the oven to 375°F. Reserve 4 tablespoons of the bread crumbs and spread the remainder on a baking sheet. Bake 10 minutes, stirring occasionally, until brown and crisp. Remove from the oven, spread on a plate and set aside to cool.

3 Rinse the zucchini thoroughly and squeeze firmly to expel as much water as possible, then pat dry between 2 clean dish towels.

4 Mix the zucchini with the reserved bread crumbs, the eggs, scallions, herbs, and some black pepper. With floured hands, form into 16 burgers, each ½ to ¾ inch thick. Coat evenly and thoroughly in the toasted bread crumbs, gently pressing them in. Leave, uncovered, in the refrigerator 1 hour.

5 Make the tzatziki by beating the yogurt until smooth, then stir in the dill and season.

6 Heat a little oil in a large skillet and fry the burgers in batches 3 to 4 minutes until brown and crisp underneath, then turn carefully and cook on the other side.

7 Meanwhile, lightly toast the rolls. Serve the burgers in the rolls with the tzatziki spooned over.

090 Tofu Kabobs

PREPARATION TIME 15 minutes, plus at least 4 hours marinating   **COOKING TIME** 20 to 30 minutes
SERVES 4

9 oz. firm tofu, drained and cut into
    1-in. cubes
8 baby onions, peeled
1 large yellow bell pepper
8 cherry tomatoes, preferably plum

TOFU MARINADE
1 tbsp. dark soy sauce
1 tbsp. dry sherry
1 tbsp. sesame oil

1 tsp. Dijon mustard
1 large garlic clove, finely chopped
2 tsp. rice wine vinegar

KABOB MARINADE
1 tbsp. sherry vinegar
1½ tsp. Dijon vinegar
1 small garlic clove, finely chopped
5 tbsp. olive oil
1½ tsp. finely chopped mixed herbs

1 Make the tofu marinade by combining the ingredients. Add the tofu and turn the cubes over
to make sure they are evenly coated. Cover and leave in the refrigerator at least 4 hours,
preferably overnight.
2 Preheat the broiler to high. Blanch the onions in boiling water 2 to 3 minutes, then drain and
refresh under cold running water. Drain again and leave to drain longer on paper towels.
3 Cook the yellow pepper in a broiler pan under the preheated broiler 10 to 15 minutes until
charred and blistered. Leave until cool enough to handle, then peel off the skin and slice the
flesh into 8 strips.
4 Make the kabob marinade by shaking the ingredients together in a screw-topped jar. Season.
5 Lift the tofu from the marinade and thread alternately onto skewers (soaked if wooden) with
the vegetables. Brush with the kabob marinade.
6 Cook on a greased broiler rack under the preheated broiler about 8 minutes, turning regularly,
until brown. Serve hot.

091 Ratatouille Pie

PREPARATION TIME 10 minutes, plus 1 hour degorging and making the pastry
COOKING TIME 1 hour 10 to 20 minutes **SERVES** 4 to 6

1 eggplant, sliced

olive oil, for frying

1 large red pepper, sliced

3 small zucchinis, quite thickly sliced

1 large onion, thinly sliced

3 garlic cloves, crushed and chopped

2 large, ripe tomatoes, chopped

a few sprigs of thyme, marjoram and parsley

leaves from a few sprigs of basil, shredded

1½ recipe quantities Pastry Dough
  (see page 104)

salt and freshly ground black pepper

1 Sprinkle the eggplant slices with salt and leave in a colander to drain for 1 hour. Rinse them thoroughly, then dry well.

2 Heat a little oil in a large skillet, add the eggplant slices, in batches if necessary, and fry until lightly browned. Remove with a fish slice and drain on kitchen paper. Add the pepper to the pan and fry for a few minutes until softened, but take care not to overcook it, then remove as before. Finally, cook the zucchinis in a little more oil, if needed, until just beginning to soften, stirring occasionally, then remove.

3 Fry the onion, adding a little more oil if necessary, and cook until softened, stirring frequently. Stir in the garlic and tomatoes for a few minutes, then return the other vegetables to the pan and add the thyme, marjoram and parsley. Season lightly, and add 2 tablespoons of oil, if desired. Cover and cook gently 30 to 35 minutes, stirring occasionally. Stir in the basil, remove from the heat and leave to cool, uncovered. Preheat the oven to 400°F.

4 Roll out two-thirds of the chilled pasty and use to line a deep 10 inch flan tin. Bake blind 15 minutes (see page 104), then remove from the oven and remove the paper and beans.

5 Roll out the remaining pastry to make a lid for the pie. Fill the pastry case with the cold vegetable mixture, carefully put the lid in place, and press the edges together. Cut a small slit in the lid. Return to the oven and bake 15 to 20 minutes until browned. Serve warm or cold.

Chapter 5

DESSERTS

My favorite desserts are fruit-based. These don't cost much because you can buy fruit offered as part of a special promotion and/or in season. If you go to farm shops or pick-your-own farms you can buy larger amounts cheaply and then preserve the surplus, by freezing, for example. Many apples can be kept just as they are, in a cool, dry place, and they last for ages.

Out of season, frozen mixed fruits, such as mixed summer berries, are better value than their fresh counterparts, and for many uses, such as the recipe shown here, work just as well. Canned fruits in natural juice are also useful. Many fruit puddings require very little or no cooking, but if you are in the mood for chocolate, one of my top choices is Chocolate-Brioche Sandwiches (see page 123), which is quick and easy.

Summer Berry Packages (see page 126)

092 Baked Apples

PREPARATION TIME 10 minutes   **COOKING TIME** 35 to 40 minutes   **SERVES** 4

4 large apples

3 tbsp. sugar

1 tsp. ground cinnamon

2 oz. marzipan, chopped

4 tbsp. chopped blanched almonds

⅓ cup dried apricots, chopped

pat of unsalted butter, chopped,
  plus extra for greasing

Greek yogurt or vanilla ice cream, to serve

1 Preheat the oven to 350°F. Using an apple corer, remove the apple cores. Then, with the
  point of a small sharp knife, cut an incision about ¾ inch deep around the circumference of
  each apple. Place the apples in a greased baking dish.

2 Mix the sugar with the cinnamon, then add the marzipan, almonds, and apricots and use to
  fill the middle of the apples. Add a small piece of butter to the top of each. Pour a little water
  into the bottom of the dish.

3 Bake in the preheated oven 35 to 40 minutes until the apples are tender.

093 Pears with Chocolate Sauce

PREPARATION TIME 5 minutes   **COOKING TIME** 8 minutes   **SERVES** 4

4 ripe but firm pears, quartered and cored
unsalted butter, melted, for brushing

CHOCOLATE SAUCE
3 oz. good-quality dark chocolate
  (at least 70% cocoa solids), chopped
½ cup cocoa powder
2 tbsp. sugar, or to taste

1 Preheat the broiler to high. Brush the pears with melted butter then cook on a broiler rack under the preheated broiler about 4 minutes on each side until warm, slightly soft, and lightly charred.

2 Meanwhile, make the sauce by melting the chocolate in ½ cup boiling water in a small bowl placed over a saucepan of hot water. Stir regularly until smooth.

3 Dissolve the cocoa powder and sugar in 2 tablespoons boiling water, then pour into the melted chocolate, stirring. Serve the pears with the warm sauce poured over.

094 Caramel Oranges

PREPARATION TIME 15 minutes   **COOKING TIME** 15 minutes   **SERVES** 4

4 large oranges
heaped ½ cup light brown sugar

vanilla ice cream, plain yogurt or crème
fraîche, to serve

1 Working over a bowl to catch any juice, carefully cut away all the orange skin and white pith. Reserve some of the skin. Cut across each orange to make about 6 slices.

2 Remove the pith from the peel, then cut the peel into very fine shreds. Blanch these in boiling water 2 to 3 minutes, until tender. Drain and dry.

3 Put the sugar and 5 tablespoons water in a small saucepan and heat slowly until the sugar dissolves, stirring gently. Bring the mixture to a boil and cook until it is a light caramel color. Pour over the oranges and set aside to chill a few hours.

4 Scatter the orange peel over the oranges and serve with scoops of vanilla ice cream, plain yogurt or crème fraîche.

095 Seared Pears with Cardamom Butter

PREPARATION TIME 15 minutes   **COOKING TIME** 8 to 12 minutes   **SERVES** 4

4 ripe but firm pears, cored, and
   thickly sliced
white or brown sugar, for sprinkling

CARDAMOM BUTTER
6 tbsp. unsalted butter, diced
1½ tsp. lemon juice
seeds from 3 crushed cardamom pods

1 Preheat the broiler to high. Make the cardamom butter by melting the butter with the lemon
   juice and cardamom seeds in a small saucepan.
2 Brush the pear slices with some of the butter and lightly sprinkle with sugar. Cook the pear
   slices on a greased broiler rack under the preheated broiler, turning occasionally and brushing
   with the butter, 4 to 6 minutes on each side until soft and beginning to caramelize. Serve the
   pears with any remaining butter spooned over.

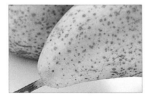

096 Chocolate–Brioche Sandwiches

PREPARATION TIME 10 minutes   **COOKING TIME** 5 minutes   **SERVES** 4

4 brioche rolls, split
good-quality apricot conserve or jam,
   for spreading

5 oz. good-quality semisweet
   chocolate, grated
vanilla ice cream, to serve (optional)

1 Preheat the broiler to medium. Spread each brioche roll half with a little conserve. Sprinkle the chocolate over the 4 bottom halves and cover with the top halves, pressing them together.
2 Cook on a broiler rack under the preheated broiler 2 to 3 minutes until the top begins to color. Turn over the sandwiches carefully and press gently with a pancake turner, then cook on the other side until the chocolate melts.
3 Serve the sandwiches straightaway, either on their own or accompanied by vanilla ice cream.

097 Fudgy Bananas

PREPARATION TIME 5 minutes   **COOKING TIME** 15 minutes   **SERVES** 4

4 bananas,

3 oz. vanilla fudge, coarsely chopped

4 tbsp. light rum

vanilla ice cream, to serve

1 Preheat the oven to 400°F. Peel the bananas and cut a slit along the length of each, then push some of the fudge into the slits. Wrap each banana in foil, sealing the edges securely.

2 Place the bananas on a baking sheet and cook in the preheated oven 10 to 15 minutes, depending on the ripeness of the bananas.

3 Remove from the oven and serve with the vanilla ice cream.

098 Plums with Cinnamon Cream

PREPARATION TIME 10 minutes   **COOKING TIME** 15 minutes   **SERVES** 4

8 large, ripe but not too soft plums,
   halved and pitted
1 tbsp. honey, warmed slightly
pat of unsalted butter, chopped

CINNAMON CREAM
1 cup heavy cream
½ tsp. cinnamon
1 tbsp. confectioners' sugar

1 Preheat the oven to 350°F.
2 Put the plum halves in a baking dish, drizzle the honey over the tops and dot with butter. Cover
   with foil and bake in the preheated oven about 15 minutes, until tender.
3 Meanwhile, make the cinnamon cream by whipping the cream to soft peaks. Mix the cinnamon
   with the sugar and fold into the cream.
4 Remove the plums from the oven and serve with the juices and cinnamon cream.

099 Summer Berry Packages

PREPARATION TIME 15 minutes, plus 30 minutes infusing   **COOKING TIME** 10 minutes   **SERVES** 4

1 lb. frozen mixed summer fruit, thawed
3 to 4 tbsp. superfine sugar
5 tbsp. orange juice
1 tbsp. lemon juice
2 tbsp. brandy

CARDAMOM CREAM
2 to 3 cardamom pods, split
about 1½ tsp. sugar, or to taste
1½ cups light or whipping cream

1 Make the cardamom cream by heating the cardamom, sugar, and cream in a heavy-bottomed saucepan until it boils. Remove from the heat, cover the pan, and leave to infuse 30 minutes. Strain, cool completely, and then chill. Preheat the oven to 350°F.

2 Divide the fruit among 4 squares of heavy-duty foil large enough to enclose the fruit.

3 Warm the brandy, superfine sugar, and fruit juices in a small saucepan until the sugar dissolves. Pour the syrup over the fruit.

4 Fold the foil loosely over the fruit and twist the edges together firmly to secure. Put the packages in a baking tray and cook in the preheated oven about 10 minutes, or until heated through.

5 Taste the cardamom cream for sweetness and adjust if necessary, and serve with the fruit packages.

100 Queen of Puddings

PREPARATION TIME 5 minutes, plus 30 minutes soaking   **COOKING TIME** 30 minutes   **SERVES** 6

1 tbsp. butter, plus extra for greasing
2½ cups milk
grated zest of ½ lemon
scant ½ cup sugar

heaped 2 cups fresh white bread crumbs
2 eggs, separated
3 tbsp. plum, black currant,
   or strawberry jam

1 Preheat the oven to 350°F. Butter 6 ramekins and place on a baking sheet.

2 Put the milk, lemon zest, and 2 tablespoons of the sugar into a heavy-bottomed saucepan and heat slowly until the sugar dissolves, stirring. Remove the pan from the heat and stir in the bread crumbs and egg yolks. Pour the mixture into the dishes and leave to soak 30 minutes.

3 Bake the puddings in the preheated oven about 20 minutes until just set. Remove from the oven and increase the temperature to 375°F.

4 Warm the jam a little in a small saucepan, then carefully spread it over the top of the puddings.

5 Whisk the egg whites until they hold soft peaks. Gradually add the remaining sugar, whisking well after each addition, until the meringue is smooth and glossy. Swirl the meringue over the puddings and bake 8 to 10 minutes until golden brown.

INDEX